CONVERGING PATHS TO TRUTH

CONVERGING PATHS TO TRUTH

THE SUMMERHAYS LECTURES ON SCIENCE AND RELIGION

EDITED BY
MICHAEL D. RHODES AND J. WARD MOODY

RELIGIOUS STUDIES CENTER
BRIGHAM YOUNG UNIVERSITY

DESERET
BOOK

Published by the Religious Studies Center, Brigham Young University, Provo, Utah, in cooperation with Deseret Book Company, Salt Lake City

http://rsc.byu.edu

© 2011 by Brigham Young University
All rights reserved.

DESERET BOOK is a registered trademark of Deseret Book Company. Visit us as DeseretBook.com

Any uses of this material beyond those allowed by the exemptions in U.S. copyright law, such as section 107, "Fair Use," and section 108, "Library Copying," require the written permission of the publisher, Religious Studies Center, 167 HGB, Brigham Young University, Provo, Utah 84602. The views expressed herein are the responsibility of the authors and do not necessarily represent the position of Brigham Young University or the Religious Studies Center.

ISBN 978-0-8425-2786-6
Retail U.S. $19.99

Cover photo: NOAO/AURA/NSF, T. Rector, H. Schweiker. Copyright WIYN Consortium, Inc., all rights reserved.

Layout and design by Jeff Wade

Library of Congress Cataloging-in-Publication Data

Converging paths to truth : the Summerhays Lectures on Science and Religion / edited by Michael D. Rhodes and J. Ward Moody.
  p. cm.
Includes bibliographical references and index.
ISBN 978-0-8425-2786-6 (hard cover : alk. paper) 1. Religion and science. 2. Church of Jesus Christ of Latter-day Saints—Doctrines. I. Rhodes, Michael D., 1946- editor. II. Moody, J. Ward (Joseph Ward), editor.

BL240.3.C684 2011
261.5'5—dc22

2011001169

Contents

Introduction Michael D. Rhodes and J. Ward Moody	vii
Faith and the Scientific Method Terry B. Ball	1
In Your Mind and in Your Heart Rodney J. Brown	17
Concerning Astronomical References Found in the Scriptures H. Kimball Hansen	37
A Brief Survey of Sir Isaac Newton's Views on Religion Steven E. Jones	61
The Quest for Truth: Science and Religion in the Best of All Worlds Robert L. Millet	79
Time in Scripture and Science: A Conciliatory Key? J. Ward Moody	101
The Scriptural Accounts of the Creation: A Scientific Perspective Michael D. Rhodes	123
Evolution and the Gospel: Seeking Grandeur in This View of Life Michael F. Whiting	151
Index	169

Composite image by Jeff Wade.

Michael D. Rhodes and J. Ward Moody

Introduction

In the fall of 2002, Briant Summerhays, J. Ward Moody, and Michael D. Rhodes proposed that Religious Education and the College of Physical and Mathematical Sciences sponsor a lecture series at BYU to promote faithful dialogue on science and religion. The goal was to create a forum where men and women of faith could share insights on how the truths of revealed religion mesh with knowledge from the sciences. The proposal was accepted, and the lecture series was named in honor of Briant's father, Hyrum Barrett Summerhays, a lifelong friend and benefactor of astronomy at BYU. The first lecture was delivered in the Harold B. Lee Library auditorium on March 21, 2003. The last was delivered in fall 2008.

The Summerhays lectures are of worth to students of both science and religion because the logic and reason that are the foundations of science are also hallmarks of true religion. Many great scientists, such as Isaac Newton and Albert Einstein, spoke and wrote freely of their religious thoughts and feelings, seeing no fundamental conflict between them and their science. It is no coincidence that many great universities which have nurtured the rise of science since the middle ages were founded and supported by religious organizations seeking truth.

The amity, though, which has existed between practitioners of science and devotees of faith has drifted in modern times toward enmity. There is a tendency now to emphasize conflict more than harmony. Sometimes people of faith are criticized as being blind, naive, or credulous, while scientists are painted as arrogant, unfeeling, or deceived. Educated dialogue between these two camps has too often been reduced to shallow platitudes or, even worse, silence.

Truth is not in conflict with itself. Religious truth is established through revelation. Scientific inquiry has uncovered many facts that have thus far stood the test of time and must also contain truth. It is incumbent upon scholars to seek insights into all truth and mesh together, where possible, its parts at their proper interface.

The opportunity to explore science in light of revealed truth is an obligation of scholars at BYU, who, in the words of Brigham Young to Karl G. Maeser, should not even "teach the alphabet or the multiplication tables without the Spirit of God."[1] We are also taught by the Savior in Doctrine and Covenants section 9 that we must first study things out in our minds before their accuracy and truth will be affirmed or denied to us. Thus it becomes our duty to actively search for truth and plead for the Holy Ghost to affirm or deny the truthfulness of our thoughts after we have had them. We discover bridges between scientific and religious knowledge best if we pursue them through study, faith, and dialogue. The Summerhays lectures are dedicated to that pursuit.

These lectures took place at or near the time of the vernal and autumnal equinoxes, approximately March 21 and September 22. The significance of these times to astronomy is apparent. It is when the days and nights are each twelve hours long, signaling the beginning of spring or fall. The vernal equinox occurs around the time of the Savior's birth and the time of the First Vision. The autumnal equinox occurs near the time when Moroni appeared to Joseph Smith for five successive tutorials, preparing him for the translation of the golden plates, which he turned over to Joseph after the last meeting. The dual significance of these dates made them the natural choice for these lectures.

A total of nine lectures were given by BYU faculty members between fall 2003 and fall 2008. We are grateful to the participants for putting their presentations in written form for inclusion in this volume. All talks presented in the series are included here with the sole exception of the excellent presentation on geological time by Dr. Bart Kowallis, whose time demands as an active researcher and department chairman were considerable.

We are indebted to Briant Summerhays for the generous support that has made these lectures possible. We are most grateful to Brent Hall and Deans Earl Woolley, Scott Sommerfeldt, Andrew Skinner, and Terry Ball for their counsel and guidance both with us and on our behalf as we have labored with the logistics of putting this series together.

It is our hope that this volume will be a worthy basis for faithful and intelligent dialogue among all interested people.

NOTES

1. Reinhard Maeser, *Karl G. Maeser: A Biography* (Provo, UT: Brigham Young University, 1928), 79.

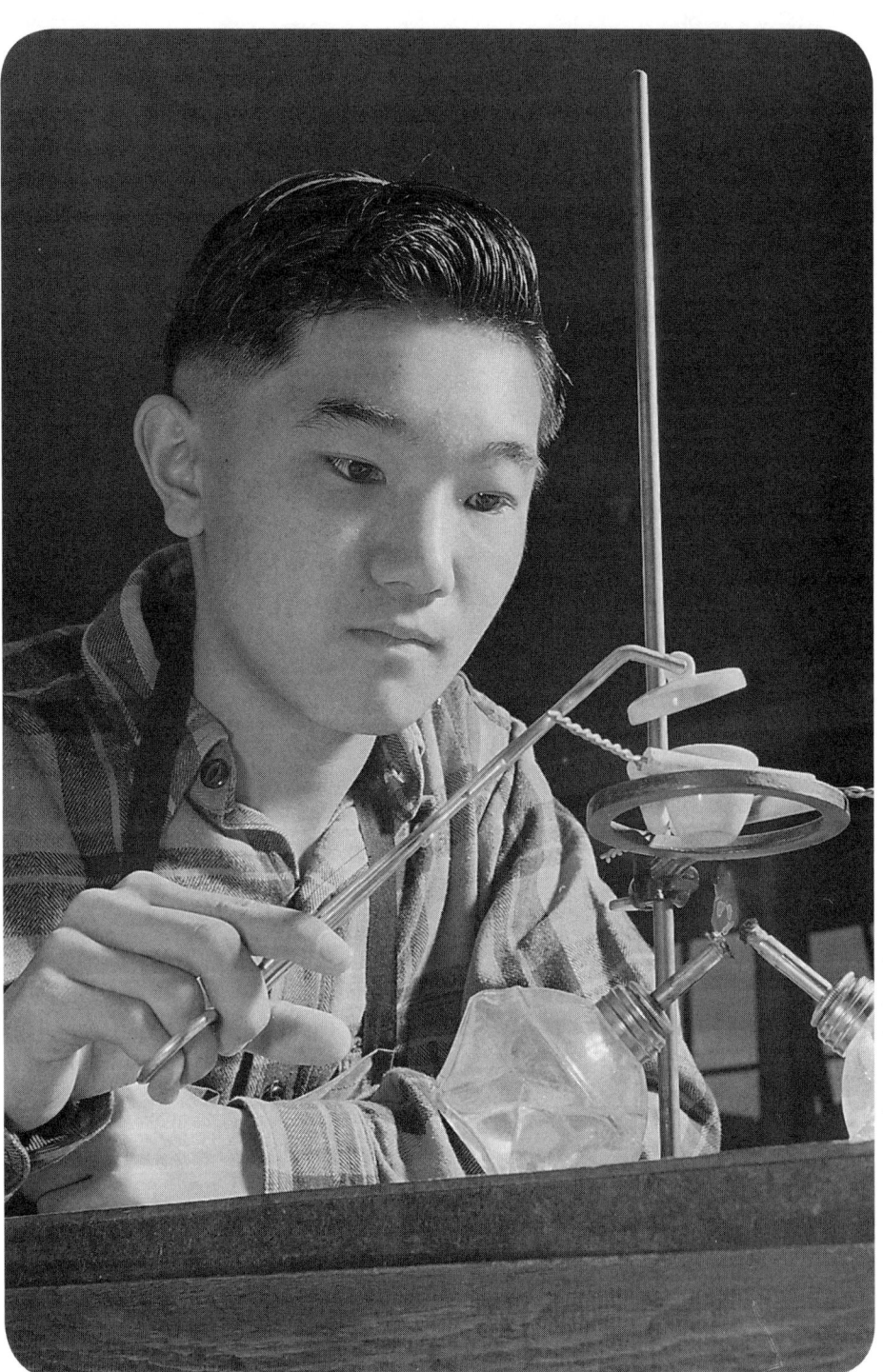

Photographer: Hikaru Iwasaka (1923–)

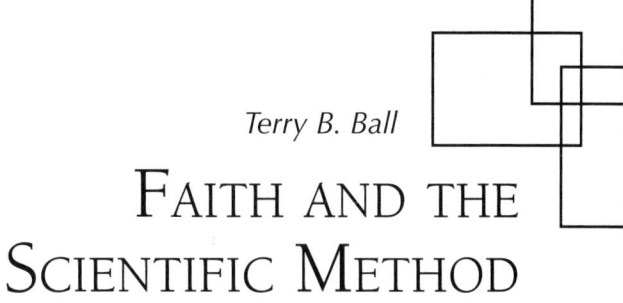

Terry B. Ball

FAITH AND THE SCIENTIFIC METHOD

THE REVEREND JOHN POLKINGHORNE, A CAMBRIDGE professor of physics and a truly world-class scientist, once expressed a dilemma experienced by many scientists who are also persons of faith with the following observation:

> There is a popular caricature which sees the scientist as ever open to the correcting power of new discovery and, in consequence, achieving the reward of real knowledge, whilst the religious believer condemns himself to intellectual imprisonment within the limits of an opinion held on a priori grounds, to which he will cling whatever facts there might be to the contrary. The one is the man of reason; the other blocks the road of honest inquiry with a barrier labelled "Incontestable revelation." If that were really so, those of us who are both scientists and religious believers . . . would be living schizophrenically, believing the impossible on Sundays and only opening our minds again on Monday mornings.[1]

In recent times, religious scientists not only have had to defend their faith in God and revelation, but also frequently

Terry B. Ball is dean of Religious Education at Brigham Young University.

find their commitment to scientific principles unjustly questioned. A Georgia judge, arguing against the teaching of evolution in school, offered an overzealous polemic that illustrates the point well. Making absurd accusations about the effect of Darwin's theories on society, the judge claimed that the "monkey mythology of Darwin is the cause of permissiveness, promiscuity, pills, prophylactics, perversions, pregnancies, abortions, pornotherapy, pollution, poisoning and proliferation of crimes of all types."[2] Such pejorative and irrational rhetoric only serves to fan the flames of hostility between science and religion while deepening the dilemma for men and women devoted to both disciplines.

Rather than adding to the tension that some individuals and institutions create between science and religion, a Brigham Young University education should help students increase their understanding and appreciation for both. As President George Albert Smith taught, "The university has a dual function, a dual aim and purpose—secular learning, the lesser value, and spiritual development, the greater. These two values must be always together, neither would be perfect without the other."[3] President Smith's counsel indicates that we should not only avoid alienating secular learning from spiritual development but also endeavor to avoid compartmentalizing and departmentalizing the two. Spiritual development can and should occur in all classes taught on the BYU campus, and secular learning may indeed find application in Religious Education classes. It is the responsibility of both faculty and students to see that President Smith's counsel is followed.

Students at BYU are fortunate to have many examples of members of the Church, past and present, who illustrate that one can indeed harmonize secular scientific learning and spiritual development. Some, for example, though trained as scientists, have provided great ecclesiastical leadership to the Church, like the Apostles John A. Widtsoe, a chemist and agronomist; James E. Talmage, a geologist; Joseph F. Merrill, a chemical engineer; Russell M. Nelson, a physician; and Richard G. Scott, a nuclear engineer.[4]

Others, while maintaining faith in the restored gospel, have made significant contributions to their scientific fields, like the physicist Philo T. Farnsworth, whose research led to the development of the television;[5] the chemist Henry Eyring, who developed the absolute rate of chemical reactions theory; and the physicist Harvey Fletcher, who pioneered the development of stereophonic sound reproduction.[6]

Today, in every department at BYU, there are individuals carrying on the legacy of these men by maintaining faith in God while serving in the Church, contributing to their disciplines, and teaching in the classrooms. Likewise, in those classrooms are many students who in the future will do the same, students who will render tremendous service in the restored gospel and who will also become renowned for their scientific contributions.

How tragic it would be if a BYU student who had the potential to become a James E. Talmage or a Henry Eyring never reached that potential because some teacher, purposefully or unwittingly, convinced that student that one must abandon faith in God in order to be a credible scientist, or conversely, that one with a testimony of the restored gospel cannot accept the tenets of science. It is imperative that as a community of learners at BYU we work to avoid such a tragedy. Every student here needs to understand, as Elder Widtsoe taught, that "the Church supports and welcomes the growth of science. . . . The religion of the Latter-day Saints is not hostile to any truth, nor to scientific search for truth."[7]

One area of persistent tension between science and religion is the relationship between faith and the scientific method. Among practicing scientists, there is a wide variety of opinions on the nature of that relationship. A review of the basic philosophies of the two most opposing schools of thought on the issue is helpful in understanding the controversy. For the sake of convenience I will refer to one extreme as scientific atheism, and the other as scientific theism.

SCIENTIFIC ATHEISM

Although the term *scientific atheism* is usually associated with the Marxist-Leninist world outlook,[8] the term can appropriately be used to describe the extreme position of those scientists who insist that there can be no relationship between faith and the scientific method. Three basic philosophies seem to lead them to this conclusion. First, they tend to believe that the scientific method is a supremely efficient and reliable tool for discovering truth. As one author describes it, they wish to view the scientific method as a "methodological threshing machine in which the flail of experiment separates the grain of truth from the chaff of error."[9]

This confidence in the efficiency and reliability of the scientific method naturally leads them to a second philosophy, which is that the scientific method by itself can answer all kinds of questions. As the nuclear chemist Jan Rydberg professed, "Science has no limits. There are no questions it should not approach."[10]

With the assurance that the scientific method can efficiently answer all kinds of questions, scientific atheists arrive at a third philosophy, which is that there is no need for faith or religion by one skilled at using the scientific method in the pursuit of truth. This philosophy was well illustrated by Pierre Simon Laplace when, as tradition has it, he responded to Napoleon's observation that he had failed to mention God in his book on the origin of the universe by saying, "Sire, I have no need for that hypothesis."[11]

Not only do scientific atheists claim no need for faith, but they also declare that any conclusions based on faith are categorically unscientific. As Brezhnev proclaimed to the Soviet Central Committee, "True science takes nothing on faith."[12] This philosophy leads its adherents to reject any superhuman source of enlightenment and to disallow any data that cannot be perceived and described by the physical senses. The final conclusion drawn by those who accept these philosophies was well illustrated by the German physicist Wilhelm Westphal when he lamented, "If there is a God, then I am very sorry to say that he has never revealed himself to me. He could have done this, in fact he should have. But he didn't. Therefore I became an atheist."[13] Rydberg confessed he had arrived at this same conclusion when he declared, "I do not need a God" and "I have no use for religion."[14]

SCIENTIFIC THEISM

In contrast to the faithless philosophies of scientific atheists, those who support the tenets of the school of thought I call *scientific theism* feel that a practitioner of the scientific method need not abandon faith. Although scientific theists are willing to agree that the scientific method is an efficient and reliable research tool, they do not believe that it is supremely or unquestionably so. Recognizing that the scientific method does not always yield unchallengeable truth, the chemist John Friedrich offered this disclaimer: "Scientists are quite often misquoted in the area of certainty. I don't believe anything is absolutely certain. Things are more or less certain depending upon the data which we have to support a given conclusion. If there is a sufficient amount of data supporting some conclusion, and no contradictory data, then we say with a certain degree of certainty that it is a true reliable conclusion."[15]

Dr. Bernard Waldman carried the thought further when he suggested that there are some scientists who, not realizing the limits of the scientific method, are "brash and very sure of what they are doing and how they have solved all the problems," but, in his discipline of physics, "the people who make the major contributions and the major breakthroughs are remarkably humble."[16] In recognizing the limits of the scientific method, scientific theists are also willing to admit that there are some questions that it simply cannot address. Willis Worcester, while serving as the dean of the College of Engineering at Virginia Polytechnic Institute, asserted that these questions often deal with issues of faith when he explained: "There are people who feel that everything can be explained on a purely scientific basis, but all of them eventually run into unanswerable questions, questions of their own origin, of the earth's origin, of their ultimate fate, which simply cannot be answered on the basis of any currently known scientific method."[17]

Some proponents of scientific theism are willing to suggest that not only can one utilize the scientific method without abandoning faith, but in reality, a kind of faith can play an important role in the scientific method itself. A former dean of the School of Science at MIT, Robert Alberty, expressed the principle this way:

> Faith is not too different from a part of the regular life of the scientist. If he didn't have faith that experiments can be reproduced and that the human mind is competent to learn more and that somehow things can be rationalized, he wouldn't go into the lab. All these acts of faith are necessary to the scientist. Maybe he doesn't look at it as faith, but it really is. This doesn't necessarily make him accept things easily, but it's wrong to think that he operates by some kind of cold calculating logic. Good scientists are highly intuitive and don't follow rigid logic. They have a great feel for things, as opposed to a detailed mastery. We present it to our students as if it were all coldly factual, but that's not the way the frontier of science is.[18]

What Alberty would call intuition, others have called inspiration. The Norwegian physicist Ole Gjotterud said, "I feel that science is the process of asking questions and trying to answer them critically, but also with inspiration."[19] This inspiration is a source of enlightenment that would be discounted by many scientific atheists because it cannot be quantified nor described in terms of the physical senses.

The willingness of scientific theists to recognize that faith and inspiration can play a role in the pursuit of truth facilitates their belief in the divine. Many confess that the further they progress in their scientific investigations, the greater their faith in, and conviction of, a supreme being becomes. Alberty said that it is this very phenomenon that "keeps God alive for scientists."[20] Atomic physicist Dr. Jules Duchesne agrees as he concludes that "the scientist's universe has become so large, so wonderful, so unexpected, he almost needs a God."[21] Perhaps the best response to the arguments of the scientific atheist was offered by the Nobel Prize-winning physicist Max Born when he simply declared, "Those who say that the study of science makes a man an atheist must be rather silly people."[22]

The experiences of students who are taught the scientific method at BYU should be similar to that of the scientific theists. They should find that their scientific education and investigations increase rather than diminish their faith. In my experience as both a teacher of religion and a researcher in a scientific field, there are three principles that have been especially beneficial in helping me recognize a harmonious relationship between faith and the scientific method.

Principle 1: Faith enhances the truths learned through the scientific method. Henry Eyring introduced this principle well when he wrote, "The scientific method which has served so brilliantly in unravelling the mysteries of this world must be supplemented by something else if we are to enjoy to the fullest the blessings that have come of the knowledge gained. It is the great mission and opportunity of religion to teach men 'the way, the truth, the life,' that they might utilize the discoveries of the laboratory to their blessing and not to their destruction."[23] Eyring's teachings suggest that when the discoveries of the scientific method become working partners with faith, each enhances the other to the blessing of humankind.

Principle 2: Faith has an application in the scientific method as well as in religion. While teaching the Zoramites, the Book of Mormon prophet Alma declared, "Faith is not to have a perfect knowledge of things; therefore if ye have faith ye hope for things which are not seen, which are true" (Alma 32:21). In other words, Alma taught that one cannot have real faith in something that is directly visible or in something that is not true. This observation leads to the question, how then does one know if something not seen is true? An answer can be found in Paul's definition of faith: "Now faith is the substance of things hoped for, the evidence of things not seen" (Hebrews 11:1). Paul's definition suggests that one can have hope for and faith in something not seen by examining the evidence of its existence. For example, though one has not seen God, the witness of the Holy Ghost can provide sufficient spiritual evidence necessary to develop faith in his existence. Moreover, many have testified that temporal evidence for the existence of God can be found in the complexity and wonders of his creations.

This principle of faith—that through observing evidence one can have confidence in the existence of something not directly seen—has found similar application in science. For example, no scientist has ever seen electrons, yet the evidence of their travel through a bubble chamber testifies of their existence.[24] In similar fashion, long before the planet Neptune was ever viewed in a telescope, Adams and Leverrier were able to predict its existence by the evidence of its gravitational influence on the planet Uranus.[25] By Paul's definition, both Adams and Leverrier exercised a principle of faith in their scientific investigations. "Now faith is the substance of things hoped for, the *evidence of things not seen*" (Hebrews 11:1; emphasis added).

After so hypothesizing or arousing ones faculties, Alma indicates that the next step, just as in the scientific method, is to perform an experiment upon the word. He explains how to conduct the experiment and evaluate the data: "Now, we will compare the word unto a seed. Now, if ye give place, that a seed may be planted in your heart" (Alma 32:28). Thus Alma instructs that the experiment should be conducted by metaphorically planting the seed of the word in one's heart. This can be interpreted as meaning that seekers of truth are to apply the teachings of Alma in their personal lives.

The third step of the scientific method, the analysis of data, is paralleled in Alma's teachings: "Behold, if it be a true seed, or a good seed, if ye do not cast it out by your unbelief, that ye will resist the Spirit of the Lord, behold, it will begin to swell within your breasts" (Alma 32:28). Thus as one evaluates the data, one recognizes that some kind of growth—a good kind of growth—has taken place.

The final step of the scientific method, that of making a conclusion, finds a cognate in Alma's paradigm for developing faith. Alma teaches that after analyzing the data of the experiment upon the word, one will come to the realization that "it must needs be that this is a good seed, or that the word is good, for it beginneth to enlarge my soul; yea, it beginneth to enlighten my understanding, yea, it beginneth to be delicious to me" (Alma 32:28). This enlarging and enlightening can be considered the spiritual data produced by the experiment.

It should be noted that this kind of spiritual evidence is very different from the physical data acceptable to the scientific method. Unlike physical data, spiritual information cannot be quantified or easily described in terms of our physical senses; rather, its observation requires the development of spiritual faculties. As a result, it may never be observed by one who has not learned how to use the spiritual senses or who limits his or her tools for pursuing truth to the scientific method. Moreover, spiritual information may manifest itself in different ways to different individuals. Thus, for those following Alma's procedure for developing faith, the spiritual data generated may not be felt or recognized by each experimenter in exactly the same way. This admission does not, however, diminish the reality or reliability of the data for those who have observed it. This may be the greatest source of frustration for scientific atheists. Because they cannot accept or recognize data in the form of spiritual witnesses and evidences, they are handicapped in their ability to learn religious truth and often deny its existence. As Paul explained to the Corinthians, "The natural man receiveth not the things of the Spirit of God: for they are foolishness unto him: neither can he know them, because they are spiritually discerned" (1 Corinthians 2:14). Biologist Hanjochem Autrum expressed a similar concept when he suggested that "science cannot find God, but the scientist can."[26]

In the remainder of his discussion on faith, Alma takes the scientific method one step further and in so doing illustrates what every good scientist should do with a newly discovered truth. He instructs that it should be nourished and cared for so that the experimenter may "reap the rewards of your faith, and your diligence" (Alma 32:43); or, using the words of Henry Eyring, "that they might utilize the discoveries of the laboratory to their blessing."[27]

The scientific method demands that the data gathered and the conclusions drawn from an experiment be reproducible by anyone who follows the procedures of the original experimenter. As Latter-day Saints, we believe that the experiment by which one can gain faith as outlined by Alma does indeed meet this criteria. And this in part helps explain the success of the great missionary program of the Church. In a sense, our missionaries challenge investigators to be "scientific" by conducting this experiment upon the word, with the promise that if they follow the procedures and carefully analyze the results, they too will come to the conclusion that God lives and that the restored gospel of Jesus Christ is true.

With the understanding of the above principles—that faith can enhance and supplement the scientific method, that the principles of faith can have application in the scientific method as well as in religion, and that the process for developing faith can be similar to the scientific method—students and educators alike can have the confidence that one need not abandon faith to be a scientist and, conversely, that a testimony of the gospel does not mandate the forsaking of science.

These principles have served me well as both a research scientist and religious educator at Brigham Young University. Over and over, my faith has informed my science, and my science has informed my faith. As an example, I would like to share a study of a passage from Isaiah 28:

> Give ye ear, and hear my voice; hearken, and hear my speech.

> Doth the plowman plow all day to sow? doth he open and break the clods of his ground?
>
> When he hath made plain the face thereof, doth he not cast abroad the fitches, and scatter the cummin, and cast in the principal wheat and the appointed barley and the rie in their place?
>
> For his God doth instruct him to discretion, and doth teach him.
>
> For the fitches are not threshed with a threshing instrument, neither is a cart wheel turned about upon the cummin; but the fitches are beaten out with a staff, and the cummin with a rod.
>
> Bread corn is bruised; because he will not ever be threshing it, nor break it with the wheel of his cart, nor bruise it with his horsemen.
>
> This also cometh forth from the Lord of hosts, which is wonderful in counsel, and excellent in working. (Isaiah 28:23–29)

This metaphor begins with a series of rhetorical questions. They make the point that a wise farmer does not spend all his time plowing his field over and over again, but rather, when the job has been adequately accomplished and the ground has been broken open and harrowed, he then proceeds to level it and sow the seeds. Five different cultivars are sown in the field of this wise farmer, each according to the manner that best suits its growth requirements and relative value.

Nutmeg flower and cumin. The first two types of seeds sown are fitches and cumin. Fitches have been variously identified as dill, vetches, carraway, and poppies, but are now usually understood to be a plant commonly called nutmeg flower or black cumin.[28] It is an annual herb of about thirty centimeters tall and has finely incised leaves. Its branches end in a showy white to blue flower possessing a five-maris corolla. The mature fruit is a pubescent capsule which contains a plethora of very small black seeds.[29] These aromatic seeds are as pungent as pepper and are thought to predate pepper in their use as a spice. In the Holy Land and Egypt, they are sprinkled over breads and pastries or added to curries and other dishes.[30] Cumin also produces small pungent seeds used as a flavoring for breads and dishes. The seeds have a taste similar to carraway seeds and have been used in folk medicine as an antispasmodic. They are also the source of an oil used in perfumes. Cumin is an annual herb of the carrot family with highly dissected leaves. It grows from one to two feet tall and produces white to pink flowers in terminal umbels.[31] Because both nutmeg flower and cumin have plentiful and relatively small seeds which do not require special spacing in their planting, the wise farmer sows them by merely throwing and scattering them over the earth.

Wheat and barley. Three different kinds of cereal grains, two wheats and one barley, were next planted in the wise farmer's fields. The first mentioned, *chittah*, was most likely the bread wheat *Triticum aestivum*, as it was the most common wheat grown at the time.[32] This remarkable wheat produces seed heads that do not spontaneously shatter, and yet with only a minimal amount of threshing they yield an abundance of naked kernels. A superior bread flour is made from its high-gluten grains. Accordingly, the wise farmer sows these valuable seeds much more cautiously. Rather than haphazardly broadcasting them about, he carefully places the valuable seeds in furrows, thus ensuring adequate germination, spacing, and watering.[33]

The next grain mentioned, barley, was also to be sown in this prudent manner, in its appointed place. Three types of barley are known to have been cultivated in biblical times: common barley, two-rowed barley, and six-rowed barley.[34] Although barley was generally considered inferior to wheat for human consumption, it was still grown for animal use at locations where the soil, moisture, and temperature would not support the less-tolerant wheats.[35]

The last cereal grain sown in this metaphor, translated as "rie," was probably a type of spelt wheat (that is, one in which the seed is firmly encased in the inflorescence bracts or "chaff" and thus not easily threshed).[36] Being an inferior wheat mostly used for animal fodder, the wise farmer planted the rie "in its place," which is better translated as "in the field's edges or borders."

Just as the wise farmer planted each cultivar in the field in the most efficacious manner, he also threshed them in the way that would yield optimal results. The delicate herbs, cumin and nutmeg flower, were not threshed with threshing sledges or cart wheels, but rather carefully beaten out with a stick. In contrast, the more robust cereal grains were threshed with a cart, but not to the extent that the kernels were crushed.[37]

Thus in his preparation, sowing, and harvesting, the wise farmer treated each cultivar in the best manner. The metaphor suggests that Jehovah acts in the same way. He has prepared for each people a place that is best for their growth and development, and placed them there in the fashion that best suits their needs and his plans for them. When it comes time for threshing (that is, chastising, separating out, or gathering in) the people, he will not do it so vigorously as to destroy them, but rather in a fashion that will maximize his harvest of saved souls.

This passage from Isaiah has become significantly more coherent and meaningful to me thanks to my scientific experience. I have enjoyed countless similar experiences of understanding in my gospel study, and my faith has played an important role in directing my scientific study. I feel to exclaim, as Isaiah, "This also cometh forth from the Lord of hosts, which is wonderful in counsel, and excellent in working" (Isaiah 28:29).

NOTES

This text combines two previously published works: Terry B. Ball, "Faith and the Scientific Method," in *Approaching a School in Zion: Proceedings of the Third Annual Laying the Foundations Symposium* (Provo, UT: Brigham Young University, 1994), 127–33, and portions of Terry B. Ball, "Isaiah's Imagery of Plants and Planting," in *Thy People Shall be My People: The 22nd Annual Sperry Symposium* (Salt Lake City: Deseret Book, 1994), 17–34.

1. John Polkinghorne, *Reason and Reality: The Relationship Between Science and Theology* (Philadelphia: Trinity Press International, 1991), 49.
2. Quoted in E. Geissler and H. Hörz, "Darwin Today—Introductory Lecture," in *Darwin Today: The Eighth Kuhlungsborn Colloquium on Philosophy and Ethical Problems of Bioscience*, ed. E. Geissler and W. Scheler (Berlin: Akademie-Verlag, 1983), 19.
3. George Albert Smith, in *Messages of the First Presidency of the Church of Jesus Christ of Latter-day Saints, 1833–1964*, comp. James R. Clark (Salt Lake City: Bookcraft, 1965), 6:234.
4. Robert L. Miller, "Science and Scientists," in *Encyclopedia of Mormonism*, ed. Daniel H. Ludlow (New York: Macmillan, 1992), 3:1272–74.
5. Ronald W. Walker and Richard W. Sadler, "History of the Church: c. 1898–1945, Transitions: Early Twentieth-Century Period," in *Encyclopedia of Mormonism*, 2:634.
6. Miller, "Science and Scientists," 1274.
7. John A. Widtsoe, *Evidences and Reconciliations* (Salt Lake City: Bookcraft, 1943), 1:129.
8. Vladimir Zots, "Atheism and the Spiritual Culture of Socialism," in *Religion in the USSR: The Truth and Falsehood* (Moscow: Social Sciences Today Editorial Board, 1986), 31.
9. Polkinghorne, *Reason and Reality*, 49.
10. Frederick E. Trinklein, *The God of Science* (Grand Rapids, MI: Eerdmans, 1971), 21.
11. Quoted in Henry Eyring, *The Faith of a Scientist* (Salt Lake City: Bookcraft, 1967), 57.
12. Stephen Fortescue, *The Communist Party and Soviet Science* (London: Macmillan, 1986), 22.
13. Trinklein, *God of Science*, 68.
14. Trinklein, *God of Science*, 68.
15. Trinklein, *God of Science*, 4.
16. Trinklein, *God of Science*, 15.
17. Trinklein, *God of Science*, 30.
18. Trinklein, *God of Science*, 19–20.
19. Trinklein, *God of Science*, 2.
20. Trinklein, *God of Science*, 61.
21. Trinklein, *God of Science*, 64.
22. Trinklein, *God of Science*, 64.

23. Eyring, *Faith of a Scientist*, 37.
24. Cyril Henderson, *Cloud and Bubble Chambers* (London: Methuen, 1970), 1–5.
25. Morton Grosser, *The Discovery of Neptune* (Cambridge, MA: Harvard University Press, 1962), 99–101.
26. Trinklein, *God of Science*, 67.
27. Eyring, *Faith of a Scientist*, 37.
28. Harold N. Moldenke and Alma L. Moldenke, *Plants of the Bible*, vol. 1 of *Chronica Botanica* (Waltham, MA: Chronica Botanica, 1952), 152.
29. Michael Zohary, *Plants of the Bible* (Tel-Aviv: Sadan Publishing House, 1982), 91.
30. Moldenke and Moldenke, *Plants of the Bible*, 152–53.
31. Moldenke and Moldenke, *Plants of the Bible*, 89; Zohary, *Plants of the Bible*, 88.
32. F. Nigel Hepper, *Baker Encyclopedia of Biblical Plants* (London: Three's Company, 1992), 85.
33. The word translated as "principle" (*sorah*) in KJV, Isaiah 28:25 is enigmatic. The Modern Language Bible translates it as "rows or furrows," as does Delitzsch, probably reading *shurah* rather than *sorah*. (Franz Delitzsch, *Biblical Commentary on the Prophecies of Isaiah* (Grand Rapids, MI: Eerdmans, 1965), 2:15. Brown suggests it is either dittographical for barley, *seorah*, or refers to some unknown kind of cereal grain. Francis Brown, *The New Brown-Driver-Briggs-Gesenius Hebrew and English Lexicon* (n.p.: Christian Copyrights, 1983), 965. In any case, the use of the verb *sam*, meaning "to put or place," suggests a careful sowing of the seeds.
34. Moldenke and Moldenke, *Plants of the Bible*, 112.
35. Hepper, *Encyclopedia of Biblical Plants*, 86.
36. The wheat referred to here, *cusemeth*, is not our modern spelt *Triticum spelta* (see Hepper, *Encyclopedia of Biblical Plants*, 86), but probably some other wheat that does not easily yield naked grains upon threshing, all of which are generically called "spelts," such as einkorn (*T. monococcum*) or emmer (*T. dicoccon*).
37. Victor L. Ludlow, *Isaiah: Prophet, Seer, and Poet* (Salt Lake City: Deseret Book, 1982), 266.

Image courtesy of Flavio Takemoto via Stock.XCHNG

Rodney J. Brown

IN YOUR MIND AND IN YOUR HEART

ABOUT TEN YEARS AGO, A MAN NAMED GYULA PALYI, whom I had never met, contacted me. He explained that in celebration of a jubilee year of the Roman Catholic Church, a series of weeklong seminars on many topics would be held simultaneously throughout Italy. He was organizing a meeting at the University of Modena on the topic "What is life? What is the origin of life? Having answered the first two questions, what are the implications?" He had been looking for a Mormon who was a scientist. I explained that I could not speak officially for The Church of Jesus Christ of Latter-day Saints and that some of my ideas would not match those of all Mormon scientists. These two disclaimers still apply.

My wife, Sandy, and I had an enjoyable week in Modena. All day long we listened to people of every scientific and religious persuasion present their thoughts on life. We heard many interesting ideas. In the evenings, we enjoyed dinners, entertainment, and discussions with people who saw things from perspectives that were often very different from ours. Sandy and I looked during that week at what I had prepared to say and refined it to become what I ended up saying, which was primarily a discussion of the plan of salvation and how we see it in relation to science.

Rodney J. Brown is dean of the College of Life Sciences at Brigham Young University.

Though I had thought about science and religion for many years, the necessity of writing and presenting my ideas focused my thoughts. Since the experience in Italy, I have had an ongoing interest in the relationship between science and religion, especially science and our religion.

WHAT IS TRUTH?

We can begin by recognizing that facts do not change. A correct answer exists for every question we could ask. We sometimes refer to eternal truths in a religious context, but eternal truths are not limited to topics generally recognized as belonging to religion. These truths are facts that are what they are and will not change. They are things as they really happened regardless of how we think they happened—things as they really are regardless of how we think they are. They do not change over time, with changing circumstances, or in any other way. They are not affected by popularity or lack of popularity. They are reality. "And truth is knowledge of things as they are, and as they were, and as they are to come" (D&C 93:24). President Brigham Young explained it this way: "Truth is calculated to sustain itself; it is based upon eternal facts and will endure, while all else will, sooner or later, perish."[1]

It is easy to convince ourselves that what we think to be true matches this definition of truth. However, no matter how carefully we try to get it right, our personal versions of what is true contain mistruths, half-truths, untruths, and so on. Things we have thought for a long time to be true are hard to discard, even when they are shown to be untrue.[2] To find the real truth requires a lot of work and it requires a level of humility that most of us find very difficult to achieve.

Another fundamental principle that we can rely on is the knowledge that God is omniscient, that he knows everything. God knows the unchangeable facts that are the ultimate answers to all our questions. He taught, "All things are present with me, for I know them all" (Moses 1:6). Furthermore, we are taught that "known unto God are all his works from the beginning of the world" (Acts 15:18). This gives us not only a solid foundation but also a clear perspective. The more we can look at things the way God looks at them, the better our chances are of understanding what we see. The Prophet Joseph Smith said in 1844, "The heavens declare the glory of God, and the firmament showeth His handiwork; and a moment's reflection is sufficient to teach every man of common intelligence, that all these are not the mere productions of *chance*, nor could they be supported by any power less than an Almighty hand."[3] Likewise, the following verses remind us that we have only a minute portion of the knowledge of God's creations. "And worlds without number have I created; and I also created them for mine own purpose; and by my Son I created them, which is mine Only Begotten. . . . But only an account of this earth, and the inhabitants thereof, give I unto you. For behold, there are many worlds that have passed away by the word of my power. And there are many that now stand, and innumerable are they unto man; but all things are numbered unto me, for they are mine and I know them" (Moses 1:33, 35). The worlds are innumerable unto man, but our best estimates are now up to around four hundred billion galaxies in the universe. This would be as a famous astronomer used to say, "billions and billions" of stars, not to mention the associated planets.

We are also told in the above verses that God's many creations were for his purposes (which we only vaguely understand), and that his Only Begotten Son created them. Humility concerning our position, wonder at the magnitude of God's creations, and awareness of the central role of Christ in all creation are essential if we are to stand on solid footing as we search for truth.

THE BREADTH OF OUR RELIGION

Our religion makes it easy to balance the theories of science with religious faith. On different occasions President Young explained the relationship of revealed religion and science this way:

> Our religion is simply the truth. It is all said in this one expression—it embraces all truth, wherever found, in all

the works of God and man that are visible or invisible to mortal eye.[4]

If you can find a truth in heaven, earth or hell, it belongs to our doctrine. We believe it; it is ours; we claim it.[5]

"Mormonism" includes all truth. There is no truth but what belongs to the gospel.[6]

It embraces every fact there is in the heavens and in the heaven of heavens—every fact there is upon the surface of the earth, in the bowels of the earth, and in the starry heavens; in fine, it embraces all truth there is in all the eternities of the Gods.[7]

In these respects we differ, from the Christian world, for our religion will not clash with or contradict the facts of science in any particular.[8]

In responding to a request to speak on our leading doctrines, John Taylor began by saying,

> In regard to our religion, I will say that it embraces every principle of truth and intelligence pertaining to us as moral, intellectual, mortal and immortal beings, pertaining to this world and the world that is to come. We are open to truth of every kind, no matter whence it comes, where it originates, or who believes in it. Truth, when preceded by the little word "all," comprises everything that has ever existed or that ever will exist and be known by and among men in time and through the endless ages of eternity; and it is the duty of all intelligent beings who are responsible and amenable to God for their acts, to search after truth, and to permit it to influence them and their acts and general course in life, independent of all bias or pre-conceived notions, however specious and plausible they may be.[9]

To members of The Church of Jesus Christ of Latter-day Saints, the search for truth and understanding is a wide-open field. We need not ever worry that we will find some truth that will clash with the gospel. No truth clashes with the gospel. But our responsibility goes beyond simple curiosity. Our desire to emulate God motivates us to understand Him and all His creations.

Since its beginning, The Church of Jesus Christ of Latter-day Saints has put a high premium on knowledge and learning. Our scriptures point out the importance of knowledge and the necessity of obtaining it by both spiritual and secular means: "The glory of God is intelligence, or, in other words, light and truth. Light and truth forsake that evil one. . . . But I have commanded you to bring up your children in light and truth" (D&C 93:36–37, 40). The scriptures go on to say, "Whatever principle of intelligence we attain unto in this life, it will rise with us in the resurrection. And if a person gains more knowledge and intelligence in this life through his diligence and obedience than another, he will have so much the advantage in the world to come" (D&C 130:18–19).

In the Doctrine and Covenants we further read:

> Teach ye diligently and my grace shall attend you, that you may be instructed more perfectly in theory, in principle, in doctrine, in the law of the gospel, in all things that pertain unto the kingdom of God, that are expedient for you to understand;
>
> Of things both in heaven and in the earth, and under the earth; things which have been, things which are, things which must shortly come to pass; things which are at home, things which are abroad; the wars and the perplexities of the nations, and the judgments which are on the land; and a knowledge also of countries and of kingdoms. (D&C 88:78–79)

As we approach truth from the direction of science and from the direction of religion, sometimes people feel caught in an uncomfortable void between faith in science and faith in religion. This leads some to think that they must abandon either science or religion to deal with apparent conflicts. President Boyd K. Packer has pointed out the necessity of balance: "Each of us must accommodate the mixture of reason and revelation in our lives. The gospel not only permits but *requires* it. An individual who concentrates on either side solely and alone will lose both balance and perspective."[10] As we learn more, and approach the truth from the directions of both religion and science, the apparent void will disappear. The destination is the same, independent of the route taken to get there. When science and religion arrive at the truth, they are at the same place and in perfect agreement with each other.

We cannot immediately know everything we would like to know. Sometimes this is very frustrating. Even partial answers can be frustrating. This presents a great temptation to jump for simple, easy explanations of things that cannot be simply or easily explained. This sometimes tempts us to avoid difficult things and instead talk about things that are not so hard to understand, or at least to explain. The world in which we live is not black and white. It is full of color and is sometimes a bit blurry. It is much clearer and more beautiful, though, if we humbly and patiently try to fit together all the pieces available from all the possible sources.

While we wait for all the pieces to come together, it is good to remember a thought attributed to F. Scott Fitzgerald: "The test of a first-rate intelligence is the ability to hold two opposed ideas in the mind at the same time, and still retain the ability to function."[11] Some find it impossible, however, to hold two differing views in their own minds and find it almost as difficult to allow differing views in the minds of others. A corollary to this thought is the observation that people tend to be most critical of those things about which they know least.

WITH ALL YOUR MIGHT

Finding the truth is not an easy thing. We might ask, "Since God knows everything, why does He not just tell us?" God could easily tell us everything we want to know and much more. Instead, he helps us learn gradually, similarly to how we try to help our children learn what we know. "For precept must be upon precept, precept upon precept; line upon line, line upon line; here a little, and there a little" (Isaiah 28:10). There is an order to acquiring knowledge that cannot be ignored. Arithmetic comes before algebra, algebra comes before calculus, and so on. Spiritual knowledge also has prerequisites. The main prerequisites for spiritual knowledge are faith and obedience.

Learning is most effective when responsibility rests more on the learner than on the teacher. Finding things out for ourselves works better than being given the answers. Elder John A. Widtsoe said, "It is not in harmony with the Gospel spirit that God, except in special cases, should reveal things that man by the aid of his natural powers may gain for himself."[12] He then cited the following verses: "Behold, you have not understood; you have supposed that I would give it unto you, when you took no thought save it was to ask me. But, behold, I say unto you, that you must study it out in your mind; then you must ask me if it be right, and if it is right I will cause that your bosom shall burn within you; therefore, you shall feel that it is right" (D&C 9:7–8). He went on to say, "So well established is this principle that in all probability many of the deepest truths contained in the writings of Joseph Smith will not be clearly understood, even by his followers, until, by the laborious methods of mortality, the same truths are established."[13] If we are to understand life and the universe in which we live, we have to work hard, using every method available to us to find the truth.

WITH ALL YOUR MIND

Science has little interest in why things are as they are, but rather in how they are and how they came to be that way.[14] Scientists like to be able to understand a thing well enough to predict what would happen under given circumstances. There is much to be learned by observing God's creations. "But ask now the beasts, and they shall teach thee; and the fowls of the air, and they shall tell thee: Or speak to the earth, and it shall teach thee: and the fishes of the sea shall declare unto thee" (Job 12:7–8).

We can learn more from studying God's creations than we can from studying the creations of other people, as good as they might be. Elder Widtsoe made some interesting comments on the wealth of knowledge God has provided for our learning. He said:

> God speaks in various ways to men. The stars, the clouds, the mountains, the grass and the soil, are all, to him who reads aright, forms of divine revelation. . . . Nowhere is this principle more beautifully illustrated and confirmed than in the rocks that constitute the crust of the earth. On them is written in simple plainness the history of the earth almost from the beginning, when the Spirit of God moved upon the face of the waters. Yet, for centuries, men saw the rocks, their forms and their adaptations to each other, without understanding the message written in them.[15]

Elder Widtsoe then went on to describe the history of the earth as read from the geological record.

Today, we could add a long list of writings to Elder Widtsoe's items. We find information and history in the genetic material of every living thing on earth. We look deep into the inside of matter to the material that forms the nucleus of atoms. We see far into space and millions of years into the past. This treasure trove of material is illuminating much of what was difficult to understand when hinted at by Joseph Smith and other prophets. This all means that there is more for us to learn than we are possibly capable of learning. It takes years for a person to gain the ability to understand even one field, let alone many fields. We therefore need to learn from and rely on each other.

Our understanding of how science works has matured over time. What was called science long ago only vaguely resembled today's science. The great philosophers—Socrates, Plato, and others—employed a simple way of discovering knowledge:

they thought about things and came to conclusions. The idea was that the mind could deduce truths on its own.[16] This method, called rationalism, led to some valuable insights, but has some serious weaknesses when used to describe the physical world. Thinking about whether the Earth is flat or round will never get to the answer without looking at the Earth.

Endless discussions and arguments intent on persuasion more than on discovery eventually led people to do what seems obvious to us today—look for evidence. At the urging of Robert Hooke, experience was proposed as being critical to the discovery of truth.[17] It then became popular to make large numbers of observations from which conclusions could be deduced. This came to be called empiricism because it is based on the use of empirical evidence. Valuable discoveries were made using this method and observation was established as the core of scientific research. Sir Isaac Newton was one of the early adopters of this new experimental philosophy.

When Albert Einstein's new ideas challenged those of Newton, and proved them wrong in some respects, a new view of how science works was emerging. Karl Popper became the spokesperson for critical rationalism.[18] The main idea behind critical rationalism is that theories about how things are can be proven false or not proven false, but can never be proven true. This realization has propelled the great surge of scientific progress in the past one hundred years.

The method used by science to find truth is appropriately called the scientific method.[19] It is based on observations and follows Popper's premise that a thing cannot be proven to be true, but can be proven to be not true. Here is how it works:

1. A theory that seems to explain all that has been observed is developed.
2. An experiment is designed to test the theory; i.e., to try to prove the theory wrong.
3. The experiment is conducted.

4. If the experiment is unable to prove the theory wrong, more experiments are designed and conducted, always trying to disprove the theory.
5. If an experiment succeeds in disproving the theory, a new theory is developed and the process begins again.

This method exposes much that is not true by slowly eliminating theories and thus causing them to be refined. It brings us incrementally closer to the truth, but never quite to it. Some theories are quickly discredited; others survive for much longer. A hierarchy of theories develops, with those that have withstood challenges for the longest time as the foundation of the pile and the newer, less tested ones exposed on the surface. All are theories that have not been proven wrong rather than facts that have been proven true. [20]

The greatest, most important asset that a scientist can have is humility. To find truth, we have to understand that we do not have the final answers, that we really do not know.[21] I will mention only a few examples of the many scientific theories that served as the best available explanation for what was observed until a better replacement was found. From our vantage point today, some of these may even look ridiculous. However, if we had lived when they were extant, they would have seemed as reasonable to us as do our present ideas. Thinking of what the explanations we accept today will look like in the future should be humbling to us.

Astronomical theories. The Ptolemaic system, favored by Aristotle and Ptolemy, had the Earth at the center of the universe with everything else rotating around it. Copernicus replaced this theory with the heliocentric system, with the planets rotating around the sun.[22] Newton's universal gravitation, with everything attracting everything else, changed the celestial logic again. Finally, for now, Einstein's ideas about general relativity has changed it all again.[23]

Aristotle's physics. Aristotle had a theory of gravity to explain why some things, like cannonballs, fall downward and other things, like steam, fall upward. He also taught that the elements that make up the Earth (earth, air, water, and fire) are different than those that make up the heavens. A system of relationships among these elements explained much that can be observed. This theory lasted for over two thousand years, but was gradually supplanted by more robust theories proposed by Galileo, Descartes, Newton, and others.

Alchemy. Aristotle's earth, air, water, and fire ideas were the foundation of the long-accepted concepts of alchemy. Aristotle taught that there is only one kind of matter, but that it can take many forms. The four fundamental forms are earth, air, water, and fire. Since all elements are of the same kind of matter, but in different forms, they should be able to be transformed into each other. Hence, great efforts were made for many years to perform transformations such as lead into gold.

Atomic theory. The concept that matter is composed of discrete units and cannot be divided into smaller units is thousands of years old. Democritus (approx. 460–370 BC) pictured such particles as the constituents of matter. They were named atoms from the Greek word for indivisible.[24] These ideas were founded on philosophical reasoning rather than experimentation and empirical observation.

Starting with the discovery of electrons by the English physicist J. J. Thompson (1856–1940), atoms began to be viewed as something other than homogeneous particles. The idea of a sun and planet relational model gradually gave way to other constructs until a model with clouds of electrons surrounding a nucleus of protons and neutrons was proposed. This model has been modified further to account for subunits of the subunits within atoms. Each of these changes was caused by the inability of a theory to withstand experimental challenges. Through all these versions of the atom, scientists explained observations in physics and chemistry based upon the theory current at their time.

Spontaneous generation. The theory of spontaneous generation said that living things appear spontaneously. This explained everything from mice appearing in a pile of dirty rags thrown in a corner to maggots on meat. It was a theory that was believed by almost everyone, including Aristotle, for hundreds of years. Then in the nineteenth century, Louis Pasteur designed and ran a simple experiment that easily proved it wrong. The current theory, which has held its own since Pasteur, is referred to as "all life from the living." Mice come from other mice, bacteria from bacteria, and so on.[25]

Miasma theory of disease. This theory started in the Middle Ages. It blamed diseases on miasma, a kind of smelly mist or vapor in the air that contained decomposed matter. During the mid-1800s, cholera outbreaks in London and Paris were blamed on miasmas. Among others, Florence Nightingale was a proponent of this theory. The miasma theory was consistent with the observations that disease was associated with poor sanitation and that sanitary improvements reduced disease. It is not consistent with the observations of microbiology that led to the current germ theory of disease.[26]

Some of these examples look almost humorous to us today. A hundred years from now, some of the things we think are true will look the same way to our descendants. However, using this strange, backward method of guessing and trying to prove our guesses wrong, we have made great progress.

Several opportunities to misuse the scientific method present themselves. Most of these are the result of forgetting or ignoring the basis of the method. For example, long accepted theories become like facts to us so we rarely see the need to test them. We need to remember, however, that the whole compilation of scientific knowledge is based on theories that continue to be tested. Some of the pieces in this pyramid will be found to be wrong and will need to be replaced.

Practicing scientists can easily fall into error by forgetting that experiments are to disprove theories, not to prove them. It is relatively easy to design experiments that fail to disprove a theory. It is a grave error to accept such failure as proof that the theory is true. This pitfall is particularly tempting to those testing theories they hope are true. The result of this error is a return to the pre–sixteenth century way of trying to explain the universe.

Another challenge we face is the limited scope of our ability to observe. We have access to only a small percentage of the spectrum. There is a limit beyond which, even with the best instruments, things are too small to see. As we look into the sky, because of the time light takes to travel, we see what far away objects looked like in the past. We can see the present only of things close to us. This makes it particularly difficult to formulate theories based on observations. Experimental science does very well considering the view we have through our small window. If we could see more, our theories would be better and science would make faster progress.

Some theories are harder to test and therefore inherently more difficult to disprove, even if they are not true. Devising tests for theories that are impossible to observe with our physical senses requires great ingenuity. Such difficult theories often require us to use evidence left from the past rather than doing controlled experiments.

Some things are completely out of range for science.[27] For example, science cannot prove the existence of God. First, science does not prove things true. It either proves them false or fails to prove them false. Second, science has a very narrow window through which to view the universe. Scientific conclusions must be based on observation. Our five senses are the only receptors available to science. We can enhance them to some extent with instruments and tools, but we are still limited to a small spectrum of physical measurements and not to any spiritual measurements.

We can, however, find the existence of God in other ways. Plenty of evidence has been given to us for this very purpose. "And behold, all things have their likeness, and all things are created and made to bear record of me, both things which are temporal, and things which are spiritual; things which are in the heavens above, and things which are on the earth, and things which are in the earth, and things which are under the earth, both above and beneath: all things bear record of me" (Moses 6:63). We also read, "Thou hast had signs enough; will ye tempt your God? Will ye say, Show unto me a sign, when ye have the testimony of all these thy brethren, and also all the holy prophets? The scriptures are laid before thee, yea, and all things denote there is a God; yea, even the earth, and all things that are upon the face of it, yea, and its motion, yea, and also all the planets which move in their regular form do witness that there is a Supreme Creator" (Alma 30:44).

Revealed religion can prove the existence of God with certainty to anyone who wants to know. Christ's answer to Peter's testimony tells us that our Father in Heaven will give us this assurance.

> When Jesus came into the coasts of Caesarea Philippi, he asked his disciples, saying, Whom do men say that I the Son of man am?
>
> And they said, Some say that thou art John the Baptist: some, Elias; and others, Jeremias, or one of the prophets.
>
> He saith unto them, But whom say ye that I am?
>
> And Simon Peter answered and said, Thou art the Christ, the Son of the living God.
>
> And Jesus answered and said unto him, Blessed art thou, Simon Bar-jona: for flesh and blood hath not revealed it unto thee, but my Father which is in heaven. (Matthew 16:13–17)

Scientists who believe in God do not believe because of scientific experiments. They believe because of the same evidence Peter received. As sure as this knowledge is to those who have it, some are not receptive to it. "But the natural man receiveth not the things of the Spirit of God: for they are foolishness unto him: neither can he know them, because they are spiritually discerned" (1 Corinthians 2:14).

WITH ALL YOUR HEART

Religion approaches an understanding of life and the universe by asking, "Why?" Though interested in how, where, when, and related questions, the greater curiosity for religion is purpose. From a religious point of view, why things are as they are is more important than how they came to be that way.[28] Even when prophets have asked for details, like Moses did, the answers are usually about purpose.

The source of information in religion is revelation. Answers are not found by trial and error, speculation, and so on, but only by communication from God. God—not man—decides what to reveal and when and to whom to reveal it. Information received by revelation has the solid attribute of being true.

The ability to separate revealed truth from less reliable information is given to everyone. Christ said, "If any man will do his will, he shall know of the doctrine, whether it be of God, or whether I speak of myself" (John 7:17).

This is both a formula for recognizing truth and for detecting untruth. Elder Bruce R. McConkie described this process as personal revelation:

> Would you like the formula to tell you how to get personal revelation? It might be written in many ways. My formula is simply this:
>
> 1. Search the scriptures.
> 2. Keep the commandments.
> 3. Ask in faith.
>
> Any person who will do this will get his heart so in tune with the Infinite that there will come into his being from the "still small voice," the eternal realities of religion. And as he progresses and advances and comes nearer to God, there will be a day when he will entertain angels, when he will see visions, and the final end is to view the face of God.[29]

Enos in the Book of Mormon, for one, tried this formula:

> And my soul hungered; and I kneeled down before my Maker, and I cried unto him in mighty prayer and supplication for mine own soul; and all the day long did I cry unto him; yea, and when the night came I did still raise my voice high that it reached the heavens. And there came a voice unto

me, saying: Enos, thy sins are forgiven thee, and thou shalt be blessed. And I, Enos, knew that God could not lie; wherefore, my guilt was swept away. And I said: Lord, how is it done? And he said unto me: Because of thy faith" (Enos 1:4–8).

Alma gave an example of the same process.

But behold, if ye will awake and arouse your faculties, even to an experiment upon my words, and exercise a particle of faith, yea, even if ye can no more than desire to believe, let this desire work in you, even until ye believe in a manner that ye can give place for a portion of my words.

Now, we will compare the word unto a seed. Now, if ye give place, that a seed may be planted in your heart, behold, if it be a true seed, or a good seed, if ye do not cast it out by your unbelief, that ye will resist the Spirit of the Lord, behold, it will begin to swell within your breasts; and when you feel these swelling motions, ye will begin to say within yourselves—It must needs be that this is a good seed, or that the word is good, for it beginneth to enlarge my soul; yea, it beginneth to enlighten my understanding, yea, it beginneth to be delicious to me.

Now behold, would not this increase your faith? I say unto you, Yea; nevertheless it hath not grown up to a perfect knowledge.

But behold, as the seed swelleth, and sprouteth, and beginneth to grow, then you must needs say that the seed is good; for behold it swelleth, and sprouteth, and beginneth to grow. And now, behold, will not this strengthen your faith? Yea, it will strengthen your faith: for ye will say I know that this is a good seed; for behold it sprouteth and beginneth to grow.

And now, behold, are ye sure that this is a good seed? I say unto you, Yea; for every seed bringeth forth unto its own likeness.

Therefore, if a seed groweth it is good, but if it groweth not, behold it is not good, therefore it is cast away.

And now, behold, because ye have tried the experiment, and planted the seed, and it swelleth and sprouteth, and beginneth to grow, ye must needs know that the seed is good. (Alma 32:27–33)

The use of the word *experiment* makes it too easy to mistake the kind of experiment described here for a scientific experiment. These experiments are designed to discover the truth of something while scientific experiments are designed to disprove things.

Because much remains unrevealed and humankind has an insatiable desire to know things, some unnecessary problems arise. Revealed information can be endlessly reformulated and elaborated upon. Such activities do not uncover additional truth, but they do generate misinformation. Hence, we hear arguments on many topics credited to God that are extrapolated beyond what he has revealed. It is at least as easy to extrapolate revealed truth beyond what is known as it is to do the same with scientific data.

CONCLUSION

People have an innate urge to know everything. God knows the unchangeable truths that are the answers to our questions. We have only a minute portion of the knowledge of what he, through his Only Begotten Son, has created for his own purposes. We are promised, however, that we can find the truth. "Yea, behold, I will tell you in your mind and in your heart, by the Holy Ghost, which shall come upon you and which shall dwell in your heart" (D&C 8:2). Humility is invaluable as we strive to learn and discover all we can. My father's favorite scripture was: "Be thou humble; and the Lord thy God shall lead thee by the hand, and give thee answer to thy prayers" (D&C 112:10).

To members of The Church of Jesus Christ of Latter-day Saints, the search for truth and understanding is a wide-open field. Mormonism embraces all truth, whatever the source or the method used to find it. We need to be careful that we do not settle too comfortably on things that we think are true without trying our very best to make sure that they are true. Science and religion both contribute in different ways to our understanding. We can see things more clearly and the world is a much more beautiful place if we use the input from both sides. When we are frustrated with partial answers, we should be very careful not to jump for easy explanations to hard questions.

In conclusion, President Howard W. Hunter said:

> It is inappropriate, especially at this university, to divide learning into secular education and religious education. Truth is, or ought to be, the object of our endeavors throughout the university, and truth is not two things; it is one. Our concern is with true science *and* true religion. Certainly the laws that govern the behavior of both molecules and men are part of the laws known and used by our Heavenly Father. God is the perfect scientist. We must not forget that our knowledge is not yet perfect. Everyone in this life must often look at matters through a glass, darkly.[30]

NOTES

Much of this chapter comes from Rodney J. Brown, *Setting the Record Straight: Mormons & Science* (Orem, UT: Millennial Press, 2008).

1. Brigham Young, in *Journal of Discourses* (London: Latter Day Saints' Book Depot, 1854–86), 14:115.
2. John Grant, *Discarded Science: Ideas That Seemed Good at the Time* (London: Facts, Figures & Fun, 2006), 8.
3. *Teachings of the Prophet Joseph Smith*, comp. Joseph Fielding Smith (Salt Lake City: Deseret Book, 1976), 56.
4. *Discourses of Brigham Young*, ed. John A. Widstoe (Salt Lake City: Deseret Book, 1954), 2.
5. Young, in *Journal of Discourses*, 13:335.
6. Young, in *Journal of Discourses*, 11:375.
7. Young, in *Journal of Discourses*, 9:149.
8. Young, in *Journal of Discourses*, 14:115.
9. John Taylor, in *Journal of Discourses*, 16:369.
10. Boyd K. Packer, "I Say unto You, Be One," in *Brigham Young University 1990–91 Devotional and Fireside Speeches* (Provo, UT: Brigham Young University, 1991), 81–92.

11. F. Scott Fitzgerald, *The Crack-Up* (New York: New Directions Books, 1956), 69.
12. John A. Widtsoe, *Joseph Smith as Scientist* (Salt Lake City: The General Board Young Men's Mutual Improvement Associations, 1908), 7.
13. Widtsoe, *Joseph Smith as Scientist*, 7.
14. Rodney J. Brown, "A Scientist's View of Life from a 'Mormon' Perspective," in *Fundamentals of Life*, ed. Gyula Palyi, Claudia Zucchi, and Luciano Caglioti (New York: Elsevier, 2002), 517–19.
15. Widtsoe, *Joseph Smith as Scientist*, 50.
16. Daniel J. Boorstin, *The Seekers: The Story of Man's Continuing Quest to Understand His World* (New York: Random House, 1998), 21.
17. James Gleick, *Isaac Newton* (New York: Pantheon Books, 2003), 62–63.
18. Karl R. Popper, *Realism and the Aim of Science* (London: Hutchinson, 1983); Herbert Keuth, *The Philosophy of Karl Popper* (Cambridge, UK: Cambridge University Press, 2004).
19. Brown, "Scientist's View of Life," 517–19.
20. Grant, *Discarded Science*, 8.
21. Richard Feynman, *The Meaning of It All* (Reading, MA: Perseus Books, 1998), 35.
22. Jack Repchek, *Copernicus' Secret: How the Scientific Revolution Began* (New York: Simon & Schuster, 2007), 8–9.
23. James Gleick, *Isaac Newton* (New York: Pantheon Books, 2003), 185–86.
24. Maitland Jones Jr., *Organic Chemistry*, 3rd ed. (New York: W. W. Norton, 2003), 1–2.
25. Daniel J. Boorstin, *The Discoverers: A History of Man's Search to Know His World and Himself* (New York: Randon House, 1983), 430.
26. Alexander Hellemans and Bryan Bunch, *The Timetables of Science: A Chronology of the Most Important People and Events in the History of Science* (New York: Simon & Schuster, 1991), 278.
27. Albert Einstein, "Science and Religion," in *The World Treasury of Physics, Astronomy, and Mathematics*, ed. Timothy Ferris (New York: Little, Brown and Company, 1991), 828–35.
28. Brown, "Scientist's View of Life," 517–19.
29. *Sermons and Writings of Bruce R. McConkie*, ed. Mark L. McConkie (Salt Lake City: Bookcraft, 1989), 157.
30. *The Teachings of Howard W. Hunter*, ed. Clyde J. Williams (Salt Lake City: Bookcraft, 1997), 183.

H. Kimball Hansen

Concerning Astronomical References Found in the Scriptures

WHILE I WAS ATTENDING THE UNIVERSITY OF CALIfornia at Berkeley, studying for a PhD in astronomy, my family and I attended church at the Claremont Ward in that city. It soon became known among the ward members what I was studying, and one Sunday after meetings an older member of the ward engaged me in conversation about what I was doing. He soon let me know that, in his opinion, the only legitimate concern for a Mormon astronomer was to find out where Kolob is located. I knew then, as I know now, that that question poses quite a number of difficulties, so I did not really tackle that problem then, nor will it be the subject of the present paper.

My purpose in this paper is to consider the overall question of astronomy (the ancient mother of the sciences) in the scriptures. I will try to lay a background picture of the wide variety of astronomical allusions, statements, references, and knowledge which can be found in our books of scripture. Later presentations in the series will build on this background.

As a starting point, consider this statement in Psalms: "The heavens declare the glory of God; and the firmament sheweth his handiwork" (19:1). This is a concise, deeply moving statement

---

H. Kimball Hansen is a professor emeritus of physics and astronomy, Brigham Young University.

of a feeling which we have all experienced. Also look at the statements of the Lord to Job concerning creation events: "Where wast thou when I laid the foundations of the earth? . . . Whereupon are the foundations fastened? or who laid the cornerstone thereof; when the morning stars sang together, and all of the sons of God shouted for joy?" (Job 38:4, 6–7). And similarly in the Doctrine and Covenants: "Let the mountains shout for joy, and all ye valleys cry aloud. . . . And let the sun, moon and morning stars sing together, and let all the sons of God shout for joy!" (128:23).

In the passages just presented, the intent seems not to be to convince us that the sun, moon, and stars actually sing together or that mountains actually shout for joy; rather, these statements seem to be intended as literary structures to enlarge our vision of what is being said—to add grandeur and impact, to emphasize the magnificence and importance of the ideas or events depicted. They also have a poetic character that impresses our ears and our minds and that aids us in retaining these things more firmly fixed in our memory. As we continue, we will see that many astronomical references in scripture are of this literary character.

On the other hand, there are also astronomical statements in scripture that relate to factual knowledge, to actual, practical, everyday, hands-on use of natural phenomena and events related to astronomy. In fact our ancestors probably knew the naked-eye sky more intimately and accurately than most of us today simply because they could *see* the sky and its splendor when they stepped outside at night, whereas we can barely even see the stars in our modern cities and towns because of light pollution.

Perhaps the most remarkable scriptural statement of this factual type is found in Helaman: "And thus, according to his word the earth goeth back, and it appeareth unto man that the sun standeth still; yea and behold, this is so; for surely it is the earth that moveth and not the sun" (12:15). This statement was made just a few years prior to the birth of Christ. For the Nephites to have such knowledge of the rotation of the earth at that time puts them distinctly ahead of the contemporary Greek astronomers and philosophers, who believed that the earth was stationary at the center of everything. Just how the Nephites became aware of this fact about the earth we do not know, but it serves as an outstanding example of factual scientific knowledge in the scriptural accounts—knowledge in full accord with our present scientific understanding of these things.

To continue this line of thought, let us now look at several other scriptural passages that give indications of a sound understanding of other astronomical or scientific facts. "He answered and said unto them, When it is evening, ye say, It will be fair weather: for the sky is red. And in the morning, It will be foul weather to day: for the sky is red and lowring" (Matthew 16:2–3). This is, of course, an aphorism that we all know today, and it was apparently common knowledge during New Testament times. You might say that this is insignificant, but it demonstrates that by careful observation over many years people can and do learn useful things about the world around them. This particular item shows how observation of an astronomical situation (sunset or sunrise) combined with meteorological conditions (clouds, haze, dust, and so on) provides a useful way of predicting general weather trends. Ancient peoples were just as intelligent as we are today; they were quite capable of observing facts in the world about them and making good use of them.

Job, speaking of God, says, "He stretcheth out the north over the empty place, and hangeth the earth upon nothing" (Job 26:7). The reference here is perhaps to the common observation that there is a region of the northern sky in which the stars never go below the horizon (the circumpolar region). The stars there never appear to touch or rest upon the horizon of the earth; they are always over empty space. And in the last phrase, does the writer of Job mean to say that the earth is not "hanging" from the stars there? Is this an intimation that the writer knew about the true condition of the earth in space, without any support above or beneath it?

God, speaking to Job, says, "Hast thou commanded the morning since thy days; and caused the dayspring to know his place?" (38:12). The modern English New International Version (NIV) translation of this verse states it this way: "Have you ever given orders to the morning, or shown the dawn its place?" (38:12, NIV). This statement seems to refer to the observed motion of the sun during the year (south on the sky in winter, north in summer) and to the way the sunrise point on the horizon tracks this motion. God here asks Job if he is the one who commands this all to occur. For our purpose it is enough to note that the writer of Job was aware of these astronomical facts. It is also relevant to note that Job may have been written at a rather early date.

Now let us look at a couple of other passages: "And it shall come to pass in that day, saith the Lord God, that I will cause the sun to go down at noon, and I will darken the earth in the clear day" (Amos 8:9). "The sun shall be turned into darkness, and the moon into blood, before that great and notable day of the Lord come" (Acts 2:20). It seems rather curious that these descriptions of the sun and moon, commonly given as signs of the coming of the Lord, are also quite accurate descriptions of the appearances of the sun and of the moon during total solar and total lunar eclipses, respectively.

Total lunar eclipses are easy to observe over large areas of the earth, and they actually occur rather frequently, so ancient people were probably well aware of them. The moon being turned to blood corresponds to the coppery appearance that the moon often has during a total lunar eclipse. This color results from the light refracted by the earth's atmosphere into the otherwise totally dark shadow. The light passing through the earth's atmosphere is altered both in direction, by refraction, and in color, by absorption. The shorter-wavelength light (violet and blue) is strongly absorbed, while the longer wavelengths (red and orange) pass through with much less attenuation. The light thus cast onto the moon is reddish in color and imparts a dull, coppery appearance to the moon during most lunar eclipses.

Astronomical References Found in the Scriptures

Total solar eclipses also occur quite frequently, but because visible totality is limited to rather narrow strips of the earth's surface, they are not commonly seen by most people. However, they are spectacular sights, and accounts of them likely circulated widely among people anciently, just as they do today. Other possibilities sometimes offered to explain a darkened sun and a bloody moon are the possible effects of great amounts of dust and smoke in the earth's atmosphere from numerous natural catastrophes such as volcanic eruptions or from large-scale nuclear warfare.

This series of lectures is meant to be on *science* and religion, not just astronomy alone, so let us here refer to an interesting passage from the book of Ecclesiastes which refers to another scientific topic. "All the rivers run into the sea; yet the sea is not full; unto the place from whence the rivers come, thither they return again" (1:7). Or in the NIV: "All streams flow into the sea, yet the sea is never full. To the place the streams come from, there they return again" (1:7, NIV). This statement reveals that the author of Ecclesiastes was aware of what we now call the water cycle of the earth. The rivers all flow to the sea, then somehow the water gets back to the sources of the rivers to flow into the sea once more. We now know that it is a process of evaporation from the seas, then precipitation as rain or snow on the land to replenish the river sources. The writer of Ecclesiastes understood the basic idea, even though he lacked knowledge of some of the details.

One last example of the factual knowledge type of scriptural statement is the often-quoted sentence from the Creation account in Genesis: "And God made two great lights; the greater light to rule the day, and the lesser light to rule the night: he made the stars also" (1:16). Anyone who has been out at night very much and who has carefully looked for the moon each night has soon realized that there are many nights when the moon is not visible at all during that night. It has apparently fallen down on its job of ruling the night. And continued observation of the situation over a full month or two reveals that the moon is visible in the nighttime sky only one-half of the time. The other half of the time it is visible in the *daylight* sky along with the sun. Whereas the sun is always visible in the full daylight sky (since the sun actually creates the day, in a sense), the moon, shining only by reflected sunlight and orbiting about the earth, is frequently nearer the sun than the earth is and so presents its shadowed side to our view, sometimes making itself fully invisible thereby. When the moon is thus between the earth and the sun, or near the positions of first and third quarter moons, it also is frequently visible above the horizon for long periods of time during daylight hours.

I believe that the Lord and Moses (the traditional author of Genesis) both fully understood all this, but for the purposes of the Genesis account, the full details were irrelevant. The important things to be stated in that account were the *purposes* for the creation of the earth and of the other bodies that make up the system of which the earth is a part, the existence of those bodies being necessary to make life possible on the earth by giving light and energy to the earth.

We have thus far looked at sufficient examples in scripture where practical astronomy (or science) is found, to establish the fact that such information is there. So let us now turn our attention to other examples where astronomical knowledge serves a largely literary purpose for the writers and prophets involved—places where astronomical knowledge, or figures of speech, are used to add a sense of wonder, exaltation, exhilaration, and grandeur or to make comparisons, similes, and metaphors which clarify, illuminate, emphasize, or enlarge the understanding of the hearer or reader.

We can start with a simple one from the Song of Solomon: "Who is she that looketh forth as the morning, fair as the moon, and clear as the sun, and terrible as an army with banners" (6:10). Or in the NIV: "Who is this that appears like the dawn, fair as the moon, bright as the sun, majestic as the stars in procession" (6:10, NIV). This is also mirrored in the Doctrine and Covenants: "That thy church may come forth out of the wilderness of darkness, and shine forth fair as the moon, clear as the sun, and terrible as an army with banners" (109:73).

The statement in the Song of Solomon stands by itself and is not closely related to the sentences preceding and following it. It only expresses Solomon's lofty, elegant, flowery description of his beloved. But the use of the same wording in the Doctrine and Covenants has a much different purpose and effect. It there describes the beauty, clarity, strength, and power of the restoration of the Lord's Church in modern times and the powerful influence which that restoration will have in preparing God's people for the momentous events of the latter days.

Then, in another vein, we have a simple natural comparison from the Book of Mormon: "And from this time forth did the Nephites gain no power over the Lamanites, but began to be swept off by them even as a dew before the sun" (Mormon 4:18). This is an effective comparison; the Nephites completely disappeared (or were annihilated), much as the sun causes the dew to quickly evaporate from every blade of grass.

We read from the Book of Mormon in its opening chapter: "And it came to pass that he saw One descending out of the midst of heaven, and he beheld that his luster was above that of the sun at noon-day. And he also saw twelve others following him, and their brightness did exceed that of the stars in the firmament" (1 Nephi 1:9–10). The glory of celestial visitors is nearly always described as brilliant, as if their normal abode were the sun itself. See also the accounts given in Moses 1 and Joseph Smith—History 1:16 in the Pearl of Great Price.

The above two verses from the Book of Mormon are the only ones that I have been able to find that make use of astronomical references of this nature. All other astronomical passages in the Book of Mormon are of a more substantive nature. We have already examined Helaman 12:15 (see also Alma 30:44); the others all refer to the events heralding Christ's birth and those occurring at his Crucifixion. In contrast, examples of the more literary type are fairly numerous in the Old Testament. Here is a small selection. "Seek him that maketh the seven stars and Orion, and turneth the shadow of death into the morning, and maketh the day dark with night: . . . The Lord is his name" (Amos 5:8) The NIV gives, "He who made the Pleiades and Orion, who turns blackness into dawn and darkens day into night, . . . the Lord is his name" (Amos 5:8, NIV). Job, in speaking of the powers of God, says, "Which maketh Arcturus, Orion, and Pleiades, and the chambers of the south" (Job 9:9). Compare also the NIV rendering here: "He is the Maker of the Bear and Orion, the Pleiades and the constellations of the south" (Job 9:9, NIV). God, in speaking to Job, asks, "Canst thou bind the sweet influences of Pleiades, or loose the bands of Orion? Canst thou bring forth Mazzaroth in his season? or canst thou guide Arcturus with his sons? Knowest thou the ordinances of heaven? canst thou set the dominion thereof in the earth?" (Job 38:31–33) Again compare with the NIV here: "Can you bind the beautiful Pleiades? Can you loose the cords of Orion? Can you bring forth the constellations in their seasons or lead out the Bear with its cubs? Do you know the laws of the heavens? Can you set up God's dominion over the earth?" (Job 38:31–33, NIV).

The objects mentioned in these passages—Orion, Pleiades, Arcturus (or the constellation Bootes), and the Bear or Ursa Major (the Big Dipper)—are some of the most prominent and beautiful of celestial objects visible in the northern hemisphere's sky. Ancient peoples knew these objects well—and the references here hark back to the idea of Psalm 19:1, that "the heavens declare the glory of God; and the firmament sheweth his handywork."

These passages from Job illustrate a dilemma inherent in this whole subject: one cannot entirely separate astronomical passages in scripture into clean, precise categories. The separation that I have made into practical versus literary is useful, but not exact. And here in these last few passages, though the literary aspects described above are present, there are also some doctrinal implications present that bear upon questions of creation and the powers of God—deep theological subjects. But because of the limited scope and content of this paper, we will have to leave the deeper questions to some other time.

In a somewhat different context, we have the astronomical comparisons concerning the degrees of glory. For example: "There are also celestial bodies, and bodies terrestrial: but the glory of the celestial is one, and the glory of the terrestrial is another. There is one glory of the sun, and another glory of the moon, and another glory of the stars: for one star differeth from another in glory. So also is the resurrection of the dead" (1 Corinthians 15:40–42).

Section 76 of the Doctrine and Covenants has a long passage (nearly forty verses) concerning these same things. I will abstract here only a few verses which mention astronomical comparisons.

> These are they whose bodies are celestial, whose glory is that of the sun, even the glory of God, the highest of all, whose glory the sun in the firmament is written of as being typical.
>
> And again, we saw the terrestrial world. . . .
>
> Wherefore, they are bodies terrestrial, and not bodies celestial, and differ in glory as the moon differs from the sun. . . .
>
> And again we saw the glory of the telestial, which glory is that of the lesser, even as the glory of the stars differs from that of the glory of the moon in the firmament. . . .
>
> But behold, and lo, we saw the glory and the inhabitants of the telestial world, that they were as innumerable as the stars in the firmament of heaven, or as the sand upon the seashore. (D&C 76:70–71, 78, 81, 109)

One could undoubtedly describe how the degrees of glory differ markedly in conditions and glory one from one another without making use of the sun, moon, and stars as metaphors and comparisons, but the use of these metaphors makes the differences immediately, emphatically clear, as well as vivid and concise. The images become definitely fixed in our minds.

Perhaps no other passages serve so well to help us see the literary, descriptive value and power of astronomical ideas in scriptural writings.

Now compare two more scriptural passages with the last sentence of the Doctrine and Covenants passage above. We go to Genesis, where we find God's promise to Abraham: "And he brought him forth abroad, and said, Look now toward the heaven, and tell the stars, if thou be able to number them: and he said unto him, So shall thy seed be" (15:5; note that the word "tell" here means "count"). "That in blessing I will bless thee, and in multiplying I will multiply thy seed as the stars of the heaven, and as the sand which is upon the seashore" (22:17). This promise is echoed in a number of other places.

If we go out into the desert or mountains, far from city lights, so that we see the sky as Abraham saw it outside his tent door, most people would exclaim that the stars one sees are innumerable. But that is simply not the case. It is really quite easy to make an accurate estimate of the total number of stars visible to the naked eye. It only requires that one make a count of the stars visible in a few sample areas of the sky (by looking through the tube from a toilet paper roll, for example) and then make a fairly simple mathematical extrapolation of those counts to what would be visible over the entire sphere of the sky, including the half below the horizon. Over years of teaching, I have had many students do this as an observing project for an astronomy class. The result is that for average eyesight, a maximum of about six thousand stars are visible, perhaps seven thousand for someone with exceptional visual acuity. That number would not be a great many descendants for Abraham to have, though the number of grains of sand upon the seashore is quite another matter. However, if we look at God's statement from a prophetic point of view, he most likely had in mind all those stars which we now know to exist which are too faint because of the vast distances involved to see without telescopic aid. Present astronomical evidence indicates that our Milky Way Galaxy contains some 100 billion (10^{11}) stars and that there is probably that same number of galaxies visible to us in the universe. That results in there being some 10^{22} stars in total in the universe, which does become comparable with the grains of sand on the seashore.

Up to this point we have considered astronomical or scientific references in a total of twenty-two different scriptural passages. This should be enough to make our main point, that meaningful references to astronomy are found throughout the standard works. And the ones that have been pointed out do not by any means approach the total number there. In a search of the standard works, looking for references to the word "sun" and making use of concordances, indexes, and some computer-aided searching of the scriptural texts, a total of approximately 190 verses were found. Of these, only 13 were in the Book of Mormon, 18 in the Doctrine and Covenants, 30 in the New Testament, and 130 in the Old Testament (35 in Ecclesiastes with its trademark phrase "under the sun"). Five verses in the parallel accounts in Moses and Abraham were dropped since they mostly duplicate ones in Genesis. Of those in the Old Testament, a fairly large fraction of the interesting references are found in the so-called wisdom literature: the books of Job, Psalms, Proverbs, Ecclesiastes, and the Song of Solomon. The word "sun" appears directly in 10 of the 22 references cited, and the sun is alluded to in two others.

REFERENCES TO CALENDAR KEEPING

There remains, however, a very interesting and important aspect of astronomy in the scriptures that we have yet to consider. That is the problem of timekeeping, or more specifically the problem of keeping and regulating an accurate and useful calendar for the ordering of a large community of people such as the Israelites. For the remainder of this discussion, we will turn our attention to that fascinating question and how it was handled in ancient times, particularly what we know about the calendar used by the Israelites of the Old Testament. Entwined with this is the practice of celebrating new moons. Be aware that in the Hebrew calendar, each month begins on the first day of the new moon, with the full moon occurring on the fourteenth or fifteenth day. (In what follows the italics are mine; it is done solely to highlight this idea of new moons.)

As an introduction to this topic, we will explore the story of David and his serving in the court of King Saul. When David finally became aware of the full depth of Saul's suspicion and enmity and realized that he was no longer safe staying in Saul's presence, he fled. After leaving the palace, he went to Jonathan, Saul's son, and in conversation with him spoke as follows: "And David said unto Jonathan, Behold to morrow is the *new moon*, and I should not fail to sit with the king at meat: but let me go, that I may hide myself in the field" (1 Samuel 20:5). The question here is, why is it that David is expected to eat with King Saul just because it is the new moon? At other places in both the Old and the New Testaments, we read of similar things. For example:

> Blow up the trumpet in the *new moon*, in the time appointed, on our solemn feast day. (Psalm 81:3).

> And it shall come to pass, that from one *new moon to another*, and from one sabbath to another, shall all flesh come to worship before me, sayeth the Lord. (Isaiah 66:23)

> Let no man therefore judge you in meat, or in drink, or in respect of an holyday, or of the *new moon*, or of the sabbath days:
> Which are a shadow of things to come. (Colossians 2:16–17)

Note well that in these passages new moons are closely associated with sabbath days and feast days, and this apparently continued into New Testament times. What is the meaning of this, and how did it come about? To find the answer, we need to go to the days of the Israelite Exodus from Egypt. There we find the following things.

The establishment of the Passover.

> And ye shall observe the feast of unleavened bread; for in this selfsame day have I brought your armies out of the land of Egypt: therefore shall ye observe this day in your generations by an ordinance for ever.
> In the *first month, on the fourteenth day* of the month at even, ye shall eat unleavened bread, until the one and twentieth day of the month at even. (Exodus 12:17–18)

> These are the feasts of the Lord, even holy convocations, which ye shall proclaim in their seasons.
> In the *fourteenth day of the first month at even* is the Lord's passover.
> And on the fifteenth day of the same month is the feast of unleavened bread unto the Lord: seven days ye must eat unleavened bread.
> In the *first day* ye shall have an *holy convocation*: ye shall do no servile work therein. (Leviticus 23:4–7)

At this point we should note the following: the Passover was a springtime festival or holy day which occurred near the time of the vernal equinox. It was related to a celebration of the first fruits of the barley harvest (and the beginning of the dry grain harvest season), which occurred in what would be our present month of April. (For the offering of first fruits, see Leviticus 23:10–12.) The Hebrews kept their calendar geared to the agricultural seasons as best they could, since they were essentially a pastoral and agricultural society with need to keep track of proper times for planting, harvesting, lambing, and so forth. The date of Passover (evening of the fourteenth day of the first month, Abib) means that it took place at the time of full moon. It is also well to be aware that another festival instituted during the time of the Exodus, the Feast of Tabernacles, was a fall (harvest) festival occurring on the fifteenth day of the seventh month, which again puts it at a time of full moon and also near the autumnal equinox. Note well also that the first day of the first month is designated a day of holy convocation, a non-work day.

Establishment of new moon festivals and sacrifices. Just to further emphasize the prevalence of this new moon idea throughout the Old Testament, we will quickly review several other references.

> Also in the day of your gladness, and in your solemn days, and in the *beginnings of your months*, ye shall blow with the trumpets over your burnt offerings, and over the sacrifices of your peace offerings; that they may be to you for a memorial before your God. I am the Lord your God. (Numbers 10:10)

> And in the *beginnings of your months* ye shall offer a burnt offering unto the Lord; two young bullocks, and one ram, seven lambs of the first year without spot;
> ... This is the burnt offering of every month *throughout the months of the year.* (Numbers 28:11, 14)

> He appointed also the king's portion of his substance for the burnt offerings, to wit, for the morning and evening burnt offerings, and the burnt offerings for the sabbaths, and for the *new moons,* and for the set feasts, as it is written in the law of the Lord. (2 Chronicles 31:3)

(In the 1979 Latter-day Saint edition of the Bible these last two passages are cross-referenced to one another on the words "beginnings of your months" and "new moons.")

And continuing on into later Old Testament times:

> Likewise the people of the land shall worship at the door of this gate before the Lord in the sabbaths and in the *new moons.*
> And the burnt offering that the prince shall offer unto the Lord in the sabbath day shall be six lambs without blemish, and a ram without blemish. . . .

> And in the day of the *new moon* it shall be a young bullock without blemish, and six lambs, and a ram: they shall be without blemish. (Ezekiel 46:3-4, 6)

> They kept also the feast of tabernacles, as it is written, and offered the daily burnt offerings by number, according to the custom, as the duty of every day required; And afterward offered the continual burnt offering, *both of the new moons, and of all the set feasts* of the Lord that were consecrated. (Ezra 3:4-5)

Though there are a fair number of further new moon references that could also be cited, these should be enough to convince us that for some reason, which I confess that I have no inkling of, it was required of the ancient Israelites to keep track of the day of the *new moon* and to celebrate that day, to consider it a *holy day*, and to *offer sacrifices* on that day. This requirement may simply be part of the extensive list of ritual performances which made up much of the Mosaic law, but it raises some perplexing calendrical problems.

Though the details are not explicitly spelled out in the Old Testament, the process of keeping track of new moon days among the Hebrews was probably similar to the practice that was common among neighboring countries and nations of that time, a practice that is known from secular historical records of those nations and from archaeological records recovered from those times. That is, the officials in charge of keeping the calendar in order went out at sunset on the day which they expected to be the first day of a new month to watch for the appearance of the first thin crescent of the moon as it became visible above the western horizon as the sun was setting and dusk began. If they did see the new crescent moon that evening, then that evening was counted as the beginning of the first day of the new month. (Days were then counted as ending and beginning at sunset.) If the crescent was not seen on the expected evening, then they watched for it the next evening. If weather interfered, then they also watched on the next evening. By the historical times in question, it was well known that the length of the month (time from new moon to new moon) was more than 29 days but less than 30 days—about 29.5 days on average—so if they missed seeing the moon on the expected evening, they could be reasonably sure that it would be visible the following evening, even if weather had been the cause for not seeing it the night before. They also, as much as possible, alternated 29- and 30-day months to keep the average length of the month near 29.5 days.

The interesting point now is that ancient Israel had two rigid calendar requirements to fulfill: First, keep the calendar year in approximate coincidence with the actual year of the seasons, to keep the first day of the year in the springtime and the Passover near the vernal equinox. Second, keep the months in exact coincidence with the phases of the moon—that is, the first day of the month coinciding with the actual day of the new moon and full moon on the 14th or 15th day of the month.

These requirements presented the Israelites with a difficult, vexing, continuing calendar-keeping problem. The sources of this problem are the following astronomical facts: the actual length of the seasonal, solar year is 365.2422 days, and the actual length of the synodic month, the month of the phases, is 29.5306 days. Both are given here to an accuracy of approximately 10 seconds, which is sufficient for our present purposes.

These times just do not fit well with one another. They are, as we say, incommensurable; that is, the larger one is not evenly divisible by the smaller. In the times that we are considering, these periods were probably known only to an accuracy of 365 days for the year and 29.5 days for the month. With these approximate values we have the following result to deal with: twelve lunar months gives $12 \times 29.5 = 354$ days, and 365 days − 354 days = 11 days. Thus every year the discrepancy between the length of 12 exact lunar months and the length of the solar year, the year of the seasons, amounts to approximately 11 days—more than one-third of a month short. This means that without any adjustment, the first day of the first month moves 11 days ahead of its original position, near the actual vernal equinox, each year. So to keep it anywhere near its correct position on a continuing basis, after three years an extra, thirteenth month needs to be inserted into the calendar to bring the lunar months back into the desired coincidence with the seasons. (This process of inserting an extra month is called intercalation.) Even with this, a three-day error still exists, and this also accumulates to the point where a thirteenth month sometimes needs to be intercalated after only two years. This whole process needs to be followed continually as long as such a lunisolar calendar is used for timekeeping purposes. It is complicated, but we can be reasonably sure from the evidence in the Old Testament that a calendar of this general type was kept by the Israelites throughout Old Testament times; however, we do not know much about its exact details until postexilic times or later. The current-day Jewish religious calendar is still of this lunisolar type.

But there is also a further problem that the ancients were not fully aware of. The 0.2422 fraction of a day in the year's length amounts to an error of 5.8 hours each year that they were not accounting for, and the 0.0306 fraction of a day for the length of the month similarly amounts to 0.73 hours per month. These may not sound like very big errors, but they accumulate month after month and year after year, and soon a whole-day error has accumulated. This means that from time to time an additional day needs to be intercalated, as well as the thirteenth month. In practice these one-day errors were inadvertently compensated for through the requirement of visually observing the new crescent moon before designating which day begins a new month. Over an extended period of time, the result would be that the months having 30 days would, by a small amount, outnumber those having only 29 days. Thus, as long as empirical designation of new moon days was the practice, these small errors would be somewhat self-adjusting. For more on intercalation, see the appendix in this article.

Below is a table showing the essential features of the Old Testament Jewish calendar, as far as we know the details. Most Bible dictionaries or encyclopedias will show a calendar similar to that shown here. Throughout most of the Old Testament, the months are most frequently referred to by their number, the first month being the one that begins at the vernal equinox. In a few places some are referred to by names which the Israelites apparently borrowed from the Canaanites. Only four of these names are presently known with certainty, and those four names appear on the chart. After the time of the exile, the Babylonian names were commonly used by the Israelites, and seven of the names shown on the calendar chart appear at various places in the Old Testament. They are marked with asterisks.

Probably also beginning after the exile, a second calendar count was used among the Israelites. This count uses the autumn month of Tishri as the first month. This calendar was more used for civil and governmental purposes, while the traditional count beginning with Nisan was principally used for religious and ceremonial purposes. The dating of the religious festivals was done in terms of the latter calendar. One should note that these two calendars were used concurrently; one calendar did not completely replace the other at some point in history. This is somewhat analogous to our using several calendars concurrently today. We have the usual calendar year of the twelve named months; we have fiscal calendars, beginning in July, October, or some other month, for business and governmental purposes; an academic calendar beginning in September is used in our schools; and, here in the West, we keep count of a "water year" beginning in October. We do not have any problems using these multiple calendars for different purposes, and it seems that ancient Israelites had no difficulties using their two calendars concurrently for their different purposes.

ASTRONOMICAL REFERENCES FOUND IN THE SCRIPTURES

OLD TESTAMENT JEWISH CALENDAR

Modern Numbers		Month Names		Modern Equivalents	Agricultural Seasons and Activities
Religious	Civil	Preexilic Canaanite	Postexilic Babylonian		
1	7	Abib	Nisan*	March–April	Spring: Later rains. Begin barley harvest. Flax harvest.
2	8	Ziv (Zif)	Iyyar	April–May	Barley harvest. Dry season begins.
3	9		Sivan*	May–June	Wheat harvest. Early figs ripen.
4	10		Tammuz	June–July	Grape harvest begins. Early grapes
5	11		Ab	July–August	Grapes, figs, and olives ripen. Olive harvest.
6	12		Elul*	August–September	Vintage begins. Dates and summer figs.
7	1	Ethanim	Tishri	September–October	Fall: Early rains, wet season. Begin plowing.
8	2	Bul	Marchesvan	October–November	Plowing. Winter figs. Wheat and barley sowing.
9	3		Chislev* (Kislev)	November–December	Sowing. Some early vineyard pruning.
10	4		Tebeth*	December–January	Rainy winter months. Snow on high ground.
11	5		Shebat*	January–February	New year for trees. Most vineyard pruning.
12	6		Adar*	February–March	Almonds blooming. Citrus fruit harvest.
13	7		Adar Sheni (2nd Adar)		Intercalary month.

CONCLUSION

If we ever reach a point in our discussions of science and religion where we think we have a pretty good match of ideas on both sides of the question, a good resolution of most of the controversies that have bedeviled us, that is when we need to be very cautious and critical of our conclusions. The reason for caution can be stated quite simply. Our experience is that religious ideas remain quite stable over long periods of time, and expectation of any large changes in the near future does not seem great. But, for science, the name of the game is change; there is constantly in the air the question, is there perhaps a better way of explaining or understanding this particular phenomenon or this particular aspect of the world or universe about us? To strive for new knowledge and new ways of understanding the world about us is ongoing and ceaseless. This does not mean that everything we know or even a significant portion of it is completely wrong; it just means that new ways of thinking about things are continually being found, that the boundaries of our knowledge are always expanding, and that new information and new understanding are continually being added to or sometimes replacing the old. And sometimes discoveries are made that cause a very large and sudden change in our view of things, new things and new ideas never even imagined before (for example, quasars and quarks). Over the fifty-some years that I have been seriously interested in astronomy, I have witnessed several such occurrences.

Thus the interface between our knowledge of religion and of science is always an active one, an interface where there are many uncertainties and much speculation. We must be constantly aware sof this and not look for or expect any easy answers. We should not be afraid to closely examine this boundary between these two important areas of knowledge, but we should do so always being aware that there are pitfalls to be avoided, on both sides.

APPENDIX

The text and the calendar chart preceding this point were part of an oral presentation given the evening of March 21, 2003. In addition to the comments made above about the process of intercalation in calendar keeping, it seems to me appropriate to give a little more detail about modern knowledge concerning this process

WHY INTERCALATION IS NEEDED

Suppose that over a long period of time we would like to keep a calendar having strictly lunar months (i.e., the months actually coinciding with the visible lunar phases) in approximate synchronization with the seasonal year, the year of 365.2422 days per year. Over three years, an error of about 3 × 11 = 33 days accumulates between the lunar calendar and the solar one. If we insert an extra thirteenth month (of 30 days) into the third year, we still have an excess of 3 days left over. This, with the 11-day error accumulating each succeeding year, will soon add up to the need to insert (intercalate) another thirteenth month into a year. As a continuing process we need to intercalate a thirteenth month every third (or second) year and do so indefinitely. This intercalation procedure is the basis of a lunisolar calendar, which is what the Old Testament Jewish calendar was.

THE METONIC CYCLE

Although the idea of intercalation was known and used in ancient calendars long before the year 380 BC, at about that time a Greek astronomer named Meton (as well as astronomers in Babylonia) became aware of a very amazing fact, as follows: 19 × 365 = 6935 days, and 235 × 29.5 = 6932.5 days. Thus 235 months (using ancient values for month and year lengths) is equal to 19 years within a difference of only 2.5 days. Using modern data for month and year lengths, the difference is only 0.0892 day, which is equal to 2 hours, 8 minutes, and 27 seconds. Truly astounding!

But for a calendar having strict lunar months we still need to use, as our foundation, the average number 29.5 days per month—that is, alternating 29- and 30-day months. For one Metonic cycle, 19 × 12 × 29.5 = 6726 days, and 19 × 365.2422 = 6939.6018 days. The difference is 213.6018 days, which is equivalent to 7.2407 months. Hence seven intercalary months need to be inserted during each 19-year period. This is usually done in the years three, six, eight, eleven, fourteen, seventeen, and nineteen of the 19-year Metonic cycle. (The modern Jewish religious calendar makes use of this pattern.) But error still remains. First, eighteen additional days must be intercalated over 95 years (five 19-year cycles), or one day about every five years, and this pattern must be continued indefinitely. These extra days can be added to months that would ordinarily be 29-day months in the regular alternation. Second, a remaining small discrepancy accumulates to another additional day after 209 years (11 metonic cycles), requiring a 1-day adjustment then and continuing at 209-year intervals thereafter. With this the resulting calendar keeps reasonably accurate synchronization with both lunar phases and the vernal equinox for a very long time period. It only needs an additional, arbitrary 1-day adjustment after something on the order of 2,700 years.

The scheme described in the preceding paragraph does not correspond in full detail to any actual lunisolar calendar in present use or any that I know of from the past. It is just a brief mathematical example of the problems posed and one way of taking account of them. Please do not consider it of any more value than that.

By comparison, the Islamic calendar, instituted by Muhammad in AD 622 and continuing in use today for religious purposes in Islamic cultures, is a strictly lunar calendar. That is, 12 lunar months constitute one complete Islamic year. There is no attempt to keep this lunar year in step with the seasonal, solar year. Hence the months of this Islamic calendar gradually drift through the seasons, each month recurring about 11 days earlier among the seasons each succeeding year, completing a full cycle in about 33 years. This is why the celebration of Ramadan (the Islamic month of fasting) occurs at different seasons as the years pass by. The months alternate 29 and 30 days as already described above. In a 30-year cycle, nineteen years have 354 days, and eleven have 355 days. This way of intercalating extra days keeps the lunar calendar in very close coincidence with the visible lunar phases over a long period. Nearly twenty-six hundred years will elapse before further adjustment is needed.

Our present-day calendar (the Gregorian calendar), which is used for civil purposes by virtually all nations today, is not a lunisolar calendar. It is a strictly solar calendar in which the year is kept in accurate coincidence with the vernal equinox by use of the addition of a leap day every fourth year—with that leap day being omitted from three leap years during each four hundred years. They are dropped from those century years which are not divisible by four hundred. No attention is paid to keeping the calendar months in coincidence with the lunar phases. The visible lunar phases thus drift through the months, and we do not use them for any significant calendrical or religious purpose.

Sir Isaac Newton, by Sir Godfrey Kneller

Steven E. Jones

A Brief Survey of Sir Isaac Newton's Views on Religion

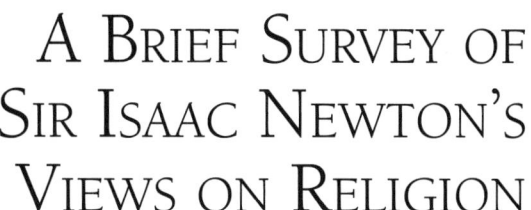

N EWTON WAS CERTAINLY ONE OF THE GREATEST SCIENtists who ever lived. He laid out the three laws of motion in his extraordinary *Principia Mathematica*. He discovered the law of universal gravitation, the famous inverse-distance-squared law. He wrote much about light and optics after performing his own original experiments on light. He invented calculus. He rejected the authority of the Greek philosopher Aristotle and promoted experiment-based science.

But it is not commonly known that Newton was also a devout Christian who wrote extensively about Christianity. We learn from his writings that he deeply studied the Bible along with writings of early Christian leaders. Notably, Newton concluded that the dogma of a triune god was false doctrine and therefore refused ordination in the Anglican Church, a most unpopular decision that almost cost him his position at Cambridge University. Newton also believed that a general apostasy from Christ's doctrines occurred early on in the history of the Christian church, and he wrote that a restoration of the Lord's church would come at some future time.

Although none of Newton's religious writings were published during his lifetime, after his death in 1727, John Conduitt,

---

Steven E. Jones is a professor emeritus of physics, Brigham Young University.

executor of Newton's will,[1] published some of his theological manuscripts. Eventually the remainder came forth when the manuscripts were auctioned off in 1936.[2] In this paper we will examine some of Newton's copious writings on religion.

Introductory Thought Experiment. Let us consider a quick thought experiment to get us thinking along Newtonian lines. Imagine a puck held by a string on a central peg so that it travels in a circular path on a "frictionless" air table like those used in air hockey games.

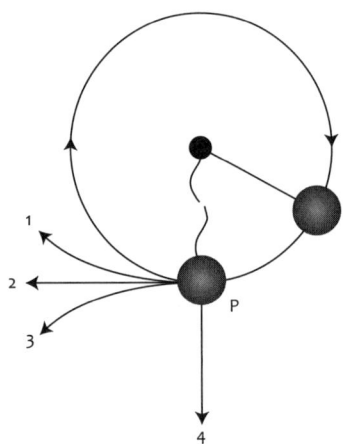

Suddenly, at point P at the bottom the string breaks. Approximately which way will the puck go—path number 1, 2, 3, or 4? When I have put this question to groups of people, the answers have included 1, 2, 3, and 4, with many not being at all sure what will happen.

But we do not do science by voting. We perform an experiment. And when we actually perform the experiment, we find that the moving puck follows path 2. It does *not* travel outward or continue in a circle.

Newton generalized the results of many such experiments in his famous three laws of motion. Newton's first law of motion can be expressed this way: An object at rest tends to stay at rest, and an object in motion tends to stay in motion with the same speed and in the same direction unless acted upon by an unbalanced force. Initially the hockey puck was constrained by the unbalanced force of the string to move in a circle. However, at the moment the string broke, it was moving in the direction of 2, and Newton's first law says that it will continue moving in that direction; this result has been confirmed by numerous actual experiments.

Experiments, careful observations, and measurements form the basis of the scientific method, and anyone can use it, Mormon or Muslim, Baptist or Buddhist. The scientific method works in repeatable fashion, independent of one's beliefs. Repeatability is the core strength of the scientific method.

During the Middle Ages, people would often answer questions by an appeal to authority. They would use the Latin term *ipse dixit*, "he himself said it," meaning that some recognized authority—Aristotle, Ptolemy, or one of the church fathers such as Augustine or Thomas Aquinas—had said it. This appeal to authority was the end of the discussion for many. Newton, however, rejected this appeal to authority and instead advocated the use of experiments and careful observations to find out what is true, which is the basis of the modern scientific method.[3] Aristotle maintained that the motion of the sun, moon, stars, and planets was circular.[4] However, Johannes Kepler, using the careful observations by Tycho Brahe, showed that they were in fact elliptical and derived equations that described their motion. A hundred years later, Newton showed that these elliptical orbits were the result of the gravitational force of the sun, which could accurately be calculated using his famous law of gravity: every point mass attracts every other point mass by a force pointing along the line intersecting both points. The force is directly proportional to the product of the two masses and inversely proportional to the square of the distance between the point masses—in equation form, $F = G((m_1 m_2)/(r^2))$.

We have important issues today that are of general concern for society. For example, is global warming real? Is it man-caused or the result of natural fluctuations in temperature? We can get the answer by repeated, careful experiments, observations, and measurements rather than by dogmatic or political statements.

A true scientist requires analysis based on experiments and observational evidence—it is not a matter of popular opinion or what some authority figure states. Questions important to society can be addressed by the scientific method, using experiments, then published in refereed journals. This system of review by knowledgeable peers was worked out during Newton's lifetime by the British Royal Academy of Sciences. It is generally considered a major step in a nascent field of science when results are finally published in established peer-reviewed venues and journals. The scientific method has served us well for about 350 years.

NEWTON IN HISTORICAL CONTEXT

The following time line places Newton in historical context with other notables.

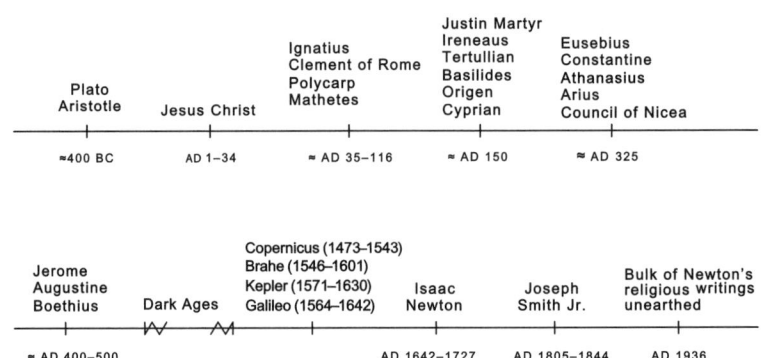

Aristotle and Plato lived about four hundred years before Christ, and their impact on Western culture has been considerable. Newton was certainly heavily influenced by Jesus Christ and the early Christian writers, for he quoted them abundantly in his writings. He took exception with some of the later Christian writers after about AD 200. Copernicus, Tycho Brahe, Kepler, and Galileo appeared on the scene just before Newton and paved the way for his research. Newton was born on the same day in 1642 that Galileo passed away, and he used many of Galileo's findings in developing his famous laws of motion. Isaac Newton died in 1727.

A MESHING OF SCIENCE AND FAITH IN GOD

Newton was both a scientist and a believer in God. He wrote *Optics*, a study of light. In this scientific treatise, he paused to ask: "Whence is it that Nature doth nothing in vain? And whence arises all that order and beauty which we see in the world? . . . Was the eye contrived without skill in optics? And the ear without knowledge of sounds?"[5] Then, in case the reader is not getting his point, he states plainly: "Does it not appear from phenomena that there is a Being incorporeal, living, intelligent, omnipresent, who in infinite space . . . sees the things themselves intimately, and thoroughly perceives them, and comprehends them wholly."[6]

In his famous *Principia*, Newton wrote: "This Being governs all things, not as the soul of the world, but as Lord over all. . . . The Supreme God is a Being eternal, infinite, absolutely perfect . . . and from his true dominion it follows that the true God is a living, intelligent, and powerful Being. . . . He is not eternity and infinity, but eternal and infinite; he is not duration or space, but he endures and is present."[7]

Newton also wrote, "When I wrote my treatise about our system I had an eye upon such principles as might work with considering men for the belief of a Deity; and nothing can rejoice me more than to find it useful for that purpose."[8] In other words, Newton hoped his scientific writings would lead people to think about and believe in God.

"In human affairs the father of a family or house is frequently taken for the common father of a kindred: here the whole creation is considered as one kindred or family so named from God, the common father of all."[9] Thus, for Newton, there was a natural meshing of science and belief in God.

In the Book of Mormon, Alma speaks of performing an individual "experiment" (he uses the same term later used by Newton) in order to learn about religious principles:

> Awake and arouse your faculties, even to an experiment upon my words, and exercise a particle of faith. . . .
>
> Now, we will compare the word unto a seed. Now, if ye give place that a seed may be planted in your heart, behold, if it be a true seed, or a good seed, if ye do not cast it out by your unbelief, that ye will resist the Spirit of the Lord,

behold, it will begin to swell within your breasts; and when you feel these swelling motions, ye will begin to say within yourselves—It must needs be that this is a good seed, or that the word is good, for it beginneth to enlarge my soul; yea, it beginneth to enlighten my understanding, yea, it beginneth to be delicious to me. . . .

And now, behold, because ye have tried the experiment, and planted the seed, and it swelleth and sprouteth, and beginneth to grow, ye must needs know that the seed is good. (Alma 32:28, 33)

Now compare this advice of Alma regarding an experiment on the word of God with this advice from Newton regarding the scriptures:

Let me therefore beg of thee not to trust to the opinion of any man concerning these things, for so it is great odds but thou shalt be deceived. Much less oughtest thou to rely upon the judgment of the multitude, for so thou shalt certainly be deceived. But search the scriptures thyself and that by frequent reading and constant meditation upon what thou readest, and earnest prayer to God to enlighten thine understanding if thou desirest to find the truth. Which if thou shalt at length attain thou wilt value above all other treasures in the world by reason of the assurance and vigour it will add to thy faith, and steady satisfaction to thy mind which he only can know how to estimate who shall experience it.[10]

It seems evident that Newton is sharing his own experience of studying the scriptures and the assurance and satisfaction the word of God brought to him, just as Alma shared his experience based on planting the word of God in his heart.

NEWTON'S KEY TO CORRECTLY UNDERSTANDING SCRIPTURE

With the foundation that Newton had obtained by reading the Bible and earnest meditation and prayer, how did he proceed to resolve other questions about religion? There were so many differing interpretations of scripture—how could one make progress in finding out the meaning intended in the Bible? Newton answers: "The first Principles of the Christian religion are founded, not on disputable conclusions, opinions, or conjectures, or on human sanctions, but on the express words of Christ and his Apostles; and we are to hold fast the form of sound words. 2 Tim. 1:13. And further, it is not enough that a proposition be true or in the express words of scripture: it must also appear to have been *taught in the days of the Apostles.*"[11] And again: "The first Principles of the Christian religion depend not on disputable conclusions. . . . Every truth, every sentence in scripture is not a fundamental article. *It must be delivered in the express words of the first teachers, and appear to have been an article taught from the beginning.*"[12] So here is Newton's approach for understanding the Bible—read the "express words of scripture" and what was "taught in the days of the Apostles."

At Cambridge University, where Newton studied, he had the writings of Ignatius, Irenaeus, Polycarp, and others of the earliest Christian writings, and he read their words in the original Latin and Greek. He quoted frequently from them and made a distinction between doctrines taught by those who lived during or soon after the Apostles and doctrines that appeared later in history.[13]

In 1661, Newton was admitted to Trinity College in Cambridge, England.[14] At that time, the college's teachings were based largely on the teachings of Aristotle and other philosophers, but Newton preferred to study the experimentalists Galileo, Copernicus, and Kepler, and he came to challenge Aristotle's teachings.[15] Shortly after he obtained his degree in April 1665, Newton left the university and for the next two years, during the pandemic known as the Great Plague, applied himself to the study of optics, gravitation, and mathematics at his mother's home in Woolsthorpe, England.[16]

Newton returned to Cambridge in 1667 to continue his studies and obtain a master of arts degree, which he obtained the following year.[17] In 1669, he was named to the Lucasian Professorship of Mathematics, an elevated position at Trinity College in the Cambridge University system.[18] Already at age twenty-six, his talents and contributions were recognized. In Newton's day, any fellow of Cambridge or Oxford had to be an ordained priest in the Anglican Church.[19] When he accepted the position, Newton promised to take holy orders in the near future but kept postponing it for several years because his personal beliefs were in disagreement with Anglican doctrine.[20] However, the pressure to take holy orders increased, and Newton considered giving up his position rather than be ordained.[21] In March 1675, he applied to King Charles for a special dispensation, and to everyone's surprise, within a month the king granted that the Lucasian Professor and all subsequent holders of the chair be exempt from holy orders.[22] Newton had expected a fight and had spent the preceding four years in preparation for it by immersing himself in the scriptures and other ancient texts, including the earliest Christian writers.[23] He filled his notebooks with scriptural quotes, from both the Old and New Testaments as well as from the earliest Christian writers.[24]

NEWTON ON THE NATURE OF THE GODHEAD

Just how did Newton apply his scientific approach in his religious studies? A prime example comes from his studies of the nature of God, which he based on the scriptures combined with the teachings of the early writers of the Christian church. Newton saw two major flaws in the Christian doctrine of the Trinity: it was unsupported from the scriptures and it was illogical.[25] Newton used scriptural passages to demonstrate that the Trinitarian doctrine was incorrect, and that the scriptures instead taught that the Father, the Son, and the Holy Ghost are separate and distinct beings, three members of the Godhead.

For example, the Son confessed that the Father was greater than him[26] and called him his God.[27] The Son also acknowledged the original prescience of all future things to be in the Father only.[28] Newton especially took exception to the Athanasian Creed, which was the first creed in which the equality of the three persons of the Trinity was explicitly stated. It is now generally accepted by scholars that Athanasius was not its author and that it most likely dates from the late fifth or even early sixth century AD—at least one hundred years after Athanasius.[29] The text of the Athanasian Creed follows:

> Whosoever will be saved, before all things it is necessary that he hold the Catholic Faith. Which Faith except everyone do keep whole and undefiled, without doubt he shall perish everlastingly. . . . The Father Uncreate, the Son Uncreate, and the Holy Ghost Uncreate. The Father Incomprehensible, the Son Incomprehensible, and the Holy Ghost Incomprehensible. The Father Eternal, the Son Eternal, and the Holy Ghost Eternal and yet they are not Three Eternals but One Eternal. As also there are not Three Uncreated, nor Three Incomprehensibles, but One Uncreated, and One Uncomprehensible. . . . So there is one Father, not three Fathers; one Son, not three Sons; one Holy Ghost, not three Holy Ghosts. And in this Trinity none is afore or after Other, None is greater or less than Another, but the whole Three Persons are Co-eternal together, and co-equal. So that in all things, as is aforesaid, the Unity in Trinity and the Trinity in Unity is to be worshipped. He therefore that will be saved, must thus think of the Trinity.[30]

For Newton this was simply not logical. He wrote, "Let them make good sense of it who are able; for my part, I can make none."[31]

NEWTON REJECTS 1 JOHN 5:7

Newton wrote a long article about the passage found in 1 John 5:7 in the King James Version, which indeed sounds a bit like the Athanasian Creed: "For there are three that bear record in heaven, the Father, the Word, and the Holy Ghost; and these three are one" (1 John 5:7). Not satisfied with this passage, Newton went back and read the text of the Vulgate as well as the original Greek. He showed that the words "in heaven, the Father, the Word, and the Holy Ghost; and these three are one" did not appear in the original Greek manuscripts. He wrote that the phrase "was neither in the ancient Versions nor in the Greek but was wholly unknown to the first churches, is most certain by an argument hinted above; namely that in all that vehement, universal, and lasting controversy about the Trinity in Jerome's time, and both before and long enough after it, this text of the Three in Heaven was never thought of. It is now in everybody's mouth and accounted the main text for the business [of supporting the Trinitarian dogma]."[32] Newton concluded, based on early texts of the Bible, that 1 John 5:7 was a later addition. He also wrote, "That apostasy was to begin by corrupting the truth about the relation of the Son to the Father in putting them equal."[33]

Scholars today agree that 1 John 5:7 is indeed spurious based on the same arguments that Newton used. The passage is not found in any early Greek manuscript, and it is not quoted by Greek Fathers, who, if they had known it, would certainly have used it in the Trinitarian controversies of the fourth century AD.[34]

NEWTON'S VIEWS OF A GENERAL APOSTASY

Newton concluded a lengthy treatise on the Book of Revelation by saying: "If you now compare all with the Apocalyptic Visions, and particularly with the flight of the woman into the wilderness and the reign of the whore of Babylon, they will very much illustrate one another: for these visions are as plain as if it had been expressly said, that the true Church shall disappear, and in her stead an idolatrous church reign in the world."[35] It is interesting to compare this with Doctrine and Covenants 86, where the Lord explains the meaning of the parable of the wheat and the tares:

> Verily, thus saith the Lord unto you my servants, concerning the parable of the wheat and the tares:
>
> Behold, verily I say, the field was the world, and the apostles were the sowers of the seed; And after they have fallen asleep the great persecutor of the church, the apostate, the whore, even Babylon, that maketh all nations to drink of her cup, in whose hearts the enemy, even Satan, sitteth to reign—behold he soweth the tares; wherefore, the tares choke the wheat and drive the church into the wilderness. (D&C 86:1-3)

Newton insisted that this was a "general Apostasy,"[36] and used such scriptures as 1 Timothy 1 and 2[37] and in particular 2 Thessalonians 2:3, which Newton translates as: "The day of the Lord shall not come except the Apostasy come first & that man of sin be revealed, the Son of perdition."[38] These, of course, are scriptures the Latter-day Saints also use to support the idea of a general apostasy.

Newton also remarked:

> Now though the unity of the Church depended upon the unity of the faith and therefore the rule of faith was unalterable, yet before the end of the second century some of the Latin churches in opposition to heretics began to add new articles to it. And after they had, by adding some articles in the language of the scriptures, made precedents for creating to themselves a creed-making authority: they began to add articles in other language than that of the scripture till they lost the primitive Apostolic rule of faith, and by the loss of it brought all into confusion.[39]

On his deathbed, Newton openly disclosed his rejection of apostate Christianity by refusing to accept the last rites of the Anglican Church.[40]

NEWTON PREDICTS A RESTORATION OF THE TRUE GOSPEL

Newton's study of the scriptures brought him to the conclusion that just as there had been a falling away, there would also be a restoration of the true church of Jesus Christ. He quoted Malachi 3 and other scriptures in his commentary that are standard scriptural passages used by Latter-day Saints in discussing the restoration:

> Behold I will send my messenger & he shall prepare the way before me & the Lord whom ye seek shall suddenly come to his temple—But who may abide the day of his coming? & who shall stand when he appeareth. Malachi 3.1, 2.[41]

> And there appeared unto them Moses & Elias & they were talking with Jesus—And (the disciples) asked him saying why say the Scribes that Elias must first come And he answered & told them Elias verily cometh first & restoreth all things. . . . Mark 9.4, 11[–]13. . . . Jesus said unto them (his disciples) Elias shall first come & restore all things. . . . Matth 17.11.[42]

> Whom the heaven must receive until the times of *restitution* of all things which God hath spoken by the mouth of *all his holy prophets since the world began*. Acts 3.21.[43]

> I will lay the Land most desolate & the pomp of her strength shall cease, & the Mountains (i.e. Cities) of Israel shall be desolate. Ezek 33.28.[44]

> Jerusalem shall become heaps, & the Mountain of the house as the high-places of the Forest: But in the last days it shall come to pass that the Mountain of the house of the Lord shall be established in the top of the Mountains & it shall be exalted above the hills &c i.e. above all other temples. Mica 3.12.[45]

So in Daniel 2 The new Jerusalem extending its dominion over the earth is represented by a great mountain which filled the whole Earth.⁴⁶

Newton found multiple examples throughout history of reformations by God:

> The worship which is due to this God we are to give to no other nor to ascribe anything absurd or contradictious to his nature or actions lest we be found to blaspheme him or to deny him or to make a step towards atheism or irreligion. . . . For as often as mankind has swerved from them, God has made a reformation. When the sons of Adam erred and the thoughts of their heart became evil continually, God selected Noah to people a new world. And when the posterity of Noah transgressed and began to invoke dead men, God selected Abraham and his posterity. And when they transgressed in Egypt God reformed them by Moses. And when they relapsed to idolatry and immorality, God sent Prophets to reform them and punished them by the Babylonian captivity. And when they that returned from captivity, mixed human inventions with the law of Moses under the name of traditions, and laid the stress of religion not upon the acts of the mind, but upon outward acts and ceremonies, God sent Christ to reform them. And when the nation received him not, God called the Gentiles. And now the Gentiles have corrupted themselves, we may expect that God in due time will make a new reformation. And in all the reformations of religion hitherto made, the religion in respect of God and our neighbor is one and the same religion . . . so that this is the oldest religion in the world.⁴⁷

Newton argued that it was the same religion that was restored from time to time by God because men deviated from this true religion. He concluded: "So then the mystery of this restitution of all things is to be found in all the Prophets:

which makes me wonder with great admiration that so few Christians of our age can find it there."[48]

CONCLUSION

Newton died on March 20, 1727, and was buried in Westminster Abby on April 4. His coffin was carried by "the Lord High Chancellor, the Dukes of Montrose and Roxborough, and the Earls of Pembroke, Sussex and Macclesfield."[49] Other great scientists buried near him include James Clerk Maxwell and Michael Faraday.

Isaac Newton was one of the world's greatest scientists. He utilized his great genius and powers of reasoning to produce his famous scientific discoveries including his laws of motion, the law of universal gravitation, studies in optics, and the invention of calculus. But he was also a devout Christian, and he brought this same intellectual genius to bear in his analysis of Christianity, and he based his beliefs on his own studies of the Bible along with the earliest Christian writers. Based on his studies, he rejected the doctrine of the Trinity and proved that it was unbiblical. He also concluded that there had been an apostasy from the true Church of Christ and that at some future time there would be a restoration.

NOTES

The author acknowledges Professor Michael D. Rhodes for a careful reading of this paper and numerous useful suggestions.

1. Michael White, *Isaac Newton: The Last Sorcerer* (Reading, MA: Addison-Wesley, 1997), 360.
2. White, *Isaac Newton*, 346.
3. Isaac Newton, *The Mathematical Principles of Natural Philosophy*, trans. Andrew Motte (Berkley University of California Press, 1946), Rule 4 in Book III, 400.
4. Aristotle, *On the Heavens*, 1.9.
5. Isaac Newton, *Opticks*, 4th ed. (London: William Innys, 1730), 344; spelling and punctuation modernized.
6. Isaac Newton, *Opticks*, 345; spelling and punctuation modernized.

7. Isaac Newton, *Principia*, ed. Stephen Hawking (Philadelphia: Running Press, 2002), 426–27.
8. Isaac Newton, Original letter from Isaac Newton to Richard Bentley, 189.R.4.47, ff. 4A-5, Trinity College Library, Cambridge, UK; found on the Newton Project website: http://www.newtonproject.sussex.ac.uk/view/texts/normalized/THEM00254; spelling and punctuation modernized.
9. Isaac Newton, *Two Notable Corruptions of Scripture (part 4: ff. 70–83)*, ms. 361(4), f. 94, New College Library, Oxford, http://www.newtonproject.sussex.ac.uk/view/texts/normalized/THEM00263; spelling and punctuation modernized.
10. Isaac Newton, *Untitled Treatise on Revelation (section 1.1)*, Yahuda Ms. 1.1, 1r–2r. Jewish National and University Library, Jerusalem, http://www.newtonproject.sussex.ac.uk/view/texts/normalized/THEM00135; spelling and punctuation modernized.
11. Isaac Newton, *Irenicum*, Keynes Ms. 3, King's College, Cambridge, 13, http://www.newtonproject.sussex.ac.uk/view/texts/normalized/THEM00003; spelling and punctuation modernized, emphasis added.
12. Newton, *Irenicum*, 25; emphasis added.
13. For example, see Isaac Newton, *Drafts on the History of the Church (Section 6)*, Yahuda Ms. 15.6, National Library of Israel, Jerusalem, http://www.newtonproject.sussex.ac.uk/view/texts/normalized/THEM00223; Isaac Newton, *Paradoxical Questions concerning the Morals & Actions of Athanasius & His Followers*, William Andrews Clark Memorial Library, Los Angeles, http://www.newtonproject.sussex.ac.uk/view/texts/normalized/THEM00117.
14. White, *Isaac Newton*, 46, 55.
15. White, *Isaac Newton*, 53.
16. White, *Isaac Newton*, 58.
17. White, *Isaac Newton*, 94–95.
18. White, *Isaac Newton*, 103.
19. White, *Isaac Newton*, 150.
20. White, *Isaac Newton*, 150.
21. White, *Isaac Newton*, 150.
22. White, *Isaac Newton*, 151.
23. White, *Isaac Newton*, 151–52.
24. See endnotes 8–10.

25. White, *Isaac Newton*, 152.
26. *Drafts on the history of the Church (Section 3)*, Yahuda Ms. 15.3, 47v., National Library of Israel, Jerusalem, http://www.newtonproject.sussex.ac.uk/view/texts/normalized/THEM00220.
27. Isaac Newton, *Drafts on the History of the Church (Section 7)*, Yahuda Ms. 15.7, 154r, National Library of Israel, Jerusalem; http://www.newtonproject.sussex.ac.uk/view/texts/normalized/THEM00237
28. Isaac Newton, *Drafts on the History of the Church (Section 3)*, Yahuda Ms. 15.3, 66r.
29. Frederick W. Norris, "Athanasian Creed," in *Encyclopedia of Early Christianity*, ed. Everett Fergusen, 2nd ed. (New York: Garland, 1997); Michael O'Carroll, "Athanasian Creed," in *Trinitas* (Wilmington, DE: Michael Glazier, 1987); *Concordia Triglotta* (St. Louis: Concordia Publishing House, 1921), 13.
30. Charles G. Herbermann and others, eds., *The Catholic Encyclopedia* (New York: The Universal Knowledge Foundation, 1907), s.v. Athanasian Creed.
31. Newton, *Two Notable Corruptions of the Scriptures (part 1: ff. 1–41)*, ms. 361(4); http://www.newtonproject.sussex.ac.uk/view/texts/normalized/THEM00261.
32. Newton, *Two Notable Corruptions of Scripture (part 1: ff. 1–41)*, ms 361(4), f. 7.
33. Isaac Newton, *Untitled Treatise on Revelation (section 1.4)*, Yahuda Ms. 1.4, 158r, Jewish National and University Library, Jerusalem, http://www.newtonproject.sussex.ac.uk/view/texts/normalized/THEM00182; spelling modernized.
34. Bruce M. Metzger, *A Textual Commentary on the Greek New Testament*, 2nd ed. (Stuttgart: German Bible Society, 1994), 647–49.
35. Isaac Newton, *Untitled Treatise on Revelation (section 1.2)*, Yahuda Ms. 1.2, 27v, National Library of Israel, Jerusalem, http://www.newtonproject.sussex.ac.uk/view/texts/normalized/THEM00137; spelling and punctuation modernized.
36. Newton, *Untitled Treatise on Revelation (section 1.2)*, Yahuda Ms. 1.2, 24r.
37. Newton, *Untitled Treatise on Revelation (section 1.2)*, Yahuda Ms. 1.2, 24r.

38. Newton, *Untitled Treatise on Revelation (section 1.2)*, Yahuda Ms. 1.2, 24v.
39. Isaac Newton, *Drafts on the History of the Church (Section 5)*, Yahuda Ms. 15.5, 92v, Jewish National and University Library, Jerusalem, http://www.newtonproject.sussex.ac.uk/view/texts/normalized/THEM00222; spelling and punctuation modernized.
40. White, *Isaac Newton*, 360.
41. Isaac Newton, *Prophesies concerning Christs 2d coming*, ASC Ms. N47 HER, James White Library, Andrews University, Berrien Springs, Michigan, USA, 8, http://www.newtonproject.sussex.ac.uk/view/texts/normalized/THEM00088; spelling modernized.
42. Newton, *Prophesies concerning Christs 2d Coming*, ASC Ms. N47 HER; spelling modernized.
43. Newton, *Prophesies concerning Christs 2d Coming*, ASC Ms. N47 HER; spelling modernized.
44. Isaac Newton, *Untitled Treatise on Revelation (section 1.1a)*, Yahuda Ms. 1.1a, 3v, Jewish National and University Library, Jerusalem, http://www.newtonproject.sussex.ac.uk/view/texts/normalized/THEM00136.
45. Newton, *Untitled Treatise on Revelation (section 1.1a)*, Yahuda Ms. 1.1a, 4r; spelling modernized.
46. Newton, *Untitled Treatise on Revelation (section 1.1a)*, Yahuda Ms. 1.1a, 3r; spelling modernized.
47. Newton, *Irenicum*, 35; spelling and punctuation modernized.
48. Yahuda MS 6, folio 12, cited in Frank E. Manuel, *The Religion of Isaac Newton* (Oxford: Clarendon, 1974), 126.
49. White, *Isaac Newton*, 360.

The Initial Act, by David Linn. © Intellectual Reserve, Inc, all rights reserved.

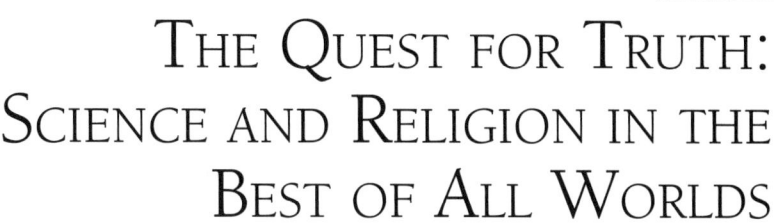

Robert L. Millet

THE QUEST FOR TRUTH: SCIENCE AND RELIGION IN THE BEST OF ALL WORLDS

I HAVE NEVER BEEN TROUBLED MUCH BY SUPPOSED DISCREPancies between what scientists have hypothesized and discovered and what prophets have pondered upon and had revealed to them. It has not been particularly difficult for me to entertain certain personal beliefs about the origin of man, the age of the earth, the dimensions of the Garden of Eden, or a universal flood while at the same time acknowledging that some of my brothers and sisters in other buildings on this campus and elsewhere would disagree with my conclusions and consider me to be naive. More times than I would like to remember, during the decade that I served as dean of Religious Education, I received phone calls from irate parents who simply could not understand why Brigham Young University was allowing organic evolution courses to be taught. They would then ask what I planned to do about it, as though I were the head of the campus thought police. I would always try to be understanding and congenial, but I would inevitably remark that such things were taught at this institution because we happened to be a university; that what was being taught was a significant dimension in the respective discipline; and that we certainly would not be doing our job very well if a science student, for example, were to

---

Robert L. Millet is a professor of ancient scripture at Brigham Young University.

graduate from Brigham Young University and be ignorant of such matters.

Sometimes, if the person had not yet chosen to hang up the phone, I would go a step further: I would point out that my first two degrees were taken at BYU in psychology, a fascinating field of study to be sure, but not necessarily one whose accepted canons were in complete harmony with my personal or denominational perspectives. While I do not believe much of what Sigmund Freud or B. F. Skinner put forth as dogma, it was critical for me as a psychology major to know and understand what they taught. No decent graduate in the behavioral sciences would be worth their salt if they left this or any other institution of higher learning ignorant of either unconscious motivation or operant conditioning.

Maybe the reason I have never been very disturbed by alternative worldviews is that I became aware at an early age that we are all of us engaged in the quest for truth, for knowledge, for understanding, for meaning, for answers to timeless questions; that no matter what our own discipline might be— whether the fine arts, the physical or mathematical sciences, the social or behavioral sciences, the humanities, or the realm of religion (and for many of us, that discipline of study we call the restored gospel)—we each "see through a glass, darkly" (1 Corinthians 13:12), to quote the Apostle Paul. That is, we do not have a complete picture. We cannot view the entire scene. We too often see things not as they really are, but rather *as we are*. In short, sometimes our findings and declarations are more autobiographical than analytical, more a reflection of our preferences and priorities and penchants than a clear declaration of pure reality, of what is. The presuppositions we incorporate and the mental maps we construct will largely determine what we see, how we see it, and, importantly, what we do not see.

One positive step each of us could take is to adopt a healthy agnosticism. Dean Rodney J. Brown at Brigham Young University has written: "Every method available should be used to increase our understanding of life and the universe in which we live. There is a complete and correct explanation of life and the universe; the information we are seeking exists. However, we are far from knowing it. There are disagreements among religions, among scientists, and between religions and scientists. This often leaves us in the void between faith in science and religious faith. As we learn more, as we approach the truth from every direction, that void will disappear."[1]

THE QUEST FOR LIGHT, NOT HEAT

Knowing and accepting the fact that what we conclude is at best an approximation of what is, I am enchanted by this familiar but fascinating passage from the Doctrine and Covenants: "And if your eye be single to my glory, your whole bodies shall be filled with light, and there shall be no darkness in you; and that body which is filled with light comprehendeth all things" (D&C 88:67). This scripture reminds me of what Danish philosopher Søren Kierkegaard taught, that "purity of heart is to will one thing."[2] If our motivation is proper, if our heart is right with the Almighty, if our desire is to contribute to the amelioration of suffering or to shine and spread light into a darkening world, and if our greatest hope is that humankind may be blessed and God glorified, then the conduit that channels light to the eye and truth to the understanding will be open and free-flowing. We will enjoy the Spirit of God in our labors, and through the influence of that member of the Godhead we will come to know "the truth of all things" (Moroni 10:5).

It is no coincidence that some of the greatest discoveries of human history have taken place during the last two centuries and, more especially, during recent decades. We should not be surprised that technological developments and medical marvels and scientific discoveries should parallel the opening of the heavens foreseen by Enoch some five millennia ago. Jehovah declared to the ancient seer, "And righteousness will I send down out of heaven; and truth will I send forth out of the earth, . . . and righteousness and truth will I cause to sweep the earth as with a flood" (Moses 7:62). Truly we are witnesses of the dual dispensation, spiritual and temporal, prophesied by Joel: "And it shall come to pass in the last days, saith God, I will pour out of my Spirit upon all flesh" (Acts 2:17; Peter paraphrasing Joel 2:28). The Light of Christ has both natural and redemptive functions. The Spirit of Jesus Christ, as it is called in the Book of Mormon (see Moroni 7:16), which serves as physical light to the eye and is the basis for law and life in the universe, is the same power by which light comes to the understanding and impressions come to the soul (see D&C 88:6–13; 84:44–47).[3]

As I have reflected on what would make me a more cooperative citizen at the university, one who could work comfortably side by side with scientists and artists and sociologists, I have drawn a few conclusions. I must admit sadly that when I was a student here at BYU and even in my first years as a faculty member, it was not uncommon for ideological grenades to be flying back and forth between the Joseph Smith Building and the Eyring Science Center. This person was labeled as godless, and that one was categorized as ignorant or naive. This faculty member hustled about to put forward his or her favorite General Authority quote, while that one relied upon a Church leader with a differing perspective. Thereby authorities were pitted against one another. Very little light, if any, was generated, but there was a great deal of heat, including much heartburn for university and college administrators. And of course the real losers during this "war of words and tumult of opinions" were the students. They admired their science teachers and valued their opinions but did not want in any way to be in opposition to what Church leaders believed and taught. They trusted their religion teachers but were not prepared to jettison their field of study. Further, such standoffs did something that for me was even more destructive: they suggested that one could not be both a competent academic and a dedicated disciple—one had to choose. And such a conclusion is tragically false. It defies everything that Brigham Young University stands for.

Maybe as Latter-day Saints we are just a little spoiled! We have so many answers to so many of life's questions that we expect to have all answers to all questions. We tend to get downright frustrated when an answer is not readily available. But not everything has yet been discovered. Not everything has yet been revealed. Consequently, we really do need to do what many of us do not do very well—deal with ambiguity. I have said to my students many times that it is as important for us to know *what we do not know* as it is for us to know what we know. If we do not yet grasp with certainty how man came to be; how long it took to create the world; how Adam and Eve were placed in the Garden of Eden; how long they lived there before they fell; what the nature of a paradisiacal, amortal existence was like within Eden or how it would affect our present efforts to measure time; when death entered the world; where dinosaurs fit into the whole program; how extensively the earth was covered by the waters in the days of Noah—if we are unsure of such matters, then perhaps we ought to be a little less eager to volunteer definitive answers, a little more tentative in our conclusions and our tendencies to crusade, and a little more patient for God to uncover truth and clarify these topics. The wisest among us learn to put the presently unexplained on the shelf for a season and move on. The wisest among us are humble enough to admit where gaps exist in our own personal knowledge and in our field of study. The wisest among us remain open to new avenues of understanding and rejoice when such insight comes.

We do our students a serious disservice if we do not explain both the strengths and limitations of our discipline or field of study. In other words, it seems only right and proper for young people to understand clearly what they *can* learn from psychology or microbiology or philosophy or mathematics, and what they *cannot* learn, which questions their discipline can answer and which ones it cannot. In that process, if we are honest and humble, we will acknowledge, as Dean Brown pointed out, that "the greater curiosity for religion is purpose," while "science explains life and the universe based on a different method of discovery. It has little interest in why things are as they are, but rather in how they are and how they came to be that way." The picture of things as they really are "is easier to see if we include what can be learned from science and from religion. The answers to many of our questions are still in the void between faith in science and religious faith. However, as we learn more, that void will disappear."[4]

THE VALUE ADDED

It is intended that there be a value-added component at Brigham Young University that has a great deal to do with the beliefs and practices of our sponsoring Church. For some, a Latter-day Saint university is an institution of higher learning that is owned and operated by The Church of Jesus Christ of Latter-day Saints, where Church standards such as the Word of Wisdom and a moral code are to be observed, where students, faculty, and staff strive to live in harmony, in the spirit of the highest of Christian virtues. I have been a part of several universities at which there are few such standards, and I for one would fight to maintain our distinctive atmosphere.

There is, of course, another way to see things. But before suggesting a different view, let me indicate how some have characterized a Christian college or university. One writer has asked,

> Is the idea of a Christian college . . . simply to offer a good education plus biblical studies in an atmosphere of piety? These are desirable ingredients, but are they the essence of the idea? After all, through religious adjuncts near a secular campus [read institutes of religion], students could be offered biblical studies and support for personal piety while they are getting a good education, without all the money and manpower and facilities and work involved in maintaining a Christian college. . . .
>
> The Christian college is distinctive . . . because we live in a secular society that compartmentalizes religion and treats it as peripheral or even irrelevant to large areas of life and thought. . . . The Christian college refuses to compartmentalize religion. It retains a unifying Christian worldview

and brings it to bear in understanding and participating in the various arts and sciences, as well as in nonacademic aspects of campus life.[5]

In short, "underlying it all [is] the basic conviction that Christian perspectives can generate a worldview large enough to give meaning to all the disciplines and delights of life and to the whole of a liberal education."[6]

It would seem then that a Latter-day Saint college or university seeks to do more than provide a healthy climate and an atmosphere suited to finding one's eternal companion (as valuable as such things are). We must constantly ask ourselves, what difference does it make that there was a Joseph Smith, a Restoration, or modern revelation? How does my religion, my way of life, my revealed worldview impact what I study or the discipline in which I spend my professional life? Am I at peace, one with myself, or do I tend to compartmentalize my life, being a scientist on Monday through Saturday and a Latter-day Saint on Sunday? Is there any tie between the scriptures I read, the sermons I hear, the prayers I utter, and the work I do in my chosen field? Is my intellectual quest merely an effort to master and acclimate myself to an academic discipline, to memorize and converse in the vocabulary of the prevailing school or trend, or rather is mine a sincere effort to seek for, tap into, acknowledge, and adapt to eternal truth, to judge and assess all things thereby?

At Brigham Young University, we have been charged to engage some of life's challenges, including hard questions, in a context of faith and mutual support, aided immeasurably by the scriptures of the Restoration and the words of living apostles and prophets. It is wrong to hide behind our religious heritage and thus neglect our academic responsibilities; there may have been a time when some faculty members at BYU excused professional incompetence in the name of religion, on the basis that BYU is different, that it is a school intent on strengthening the commitment of young Latter-day Saints. This was commendable but insufficient. It is just as myopic, however, to hide behind academics and thus cover our own spiritual incompetence. We can be thoroughly competent disciples and thoroughly competent professionals. We do not hide behind our religion, but rather we come to see all things through the lenses of our religion. "We are not only to teach purely gospel subjects by the power of the Spirit," Elder Marion G. Romney counseled. "We are also to teach secular subjects by the power of the Spirit, and we are obligated to interpret the content of secular subjects *in the light of revealed truth*. This purpose is the only sufficient justification for spending Church money to maintain this institution."[7]

Thirty years ago Professor Allen Bergin was asked to chair a session of the American Psychological Association meetings in Los Angeles. He called me and a colleague of mine in Florida and invited us to present a paper titled "Religious Values in Psychotherapy." We accepted, knowing that we had several months to prepare. I began pushing my friend early, suggesting regularly that we get together, organize ourselves, and make arrangements for the writing of the paper. Being an extremely busy man, he put me off again and again. To make a long and painful story short, I found myself on the plane to Los Angeles saying, "Charley, we've just got to pull something together. This is big time. We can't wing it; we can't go into that meeting totally unprepared." He agreed and reached into his coat pocket at that point, pulled out an envelope, and we began making a few notes.

The presentation was at best okay. It was not spectacular, not excellent, not even very good. It was okay. I was embarrassed and wished that we had spent at least some time ordering our thoughts. The funny thing is, a number of people surrounded us after the session to ask questions, to inquire after our own religious beliefs, and to request further information. Quite a few asked me if they could receive copies of our presentation. I was sorely tempted to indicate that all they needed to do was photocopy the envelope, but I did not yield! The occasion taught me something, a lesson that is not easily forgotten: people out there need and want what we have.

Often they are not even aware of what that something is; they just want it! Brigham Young University has been established to assist the Church in extending to Latter-day Saints and to men and women of good will everywhere the very glory of God, but we must be in a position—be competent as well as humble—to let that kindly light shine. In other words, the glorious light of revealed truth must be allowed to shine forth undimmed and unrefracted.

THE QUEST FOR UNITY

Certain disciplines lend themselves quite readily to the consideration of academic matters in the light of the restored gospel. Discussions of this sort will often be rather spontaneous and unpremeditated. With some areas of study this will be more difficult, and efforts to introduce religion or religious principles may be perceived as unnatural or contrived. It is not that we must create a Church-centered chemistry or a Mormon mathematics or a Latter-day Saint linguistics at BYU. More important, we must live in such a way that students and faculty have no reason to wonder where we stand on matters of faith and commitment. Obviously when we cultivate the spirit of inspiration on this campus, the truths of the gospel will be taught and learned more effectively; edification will be the order of the day. But the principle extends beyond the teaching of religion or the explanation of gospel precepts. It has much to do with how we teach, research, write, discover, display, and apply truths in all fields of study. Students who attend a calculus class taught by an instructor imbued with the Spirit of God will be richly rewarded, even if a religious principle is never mentioned. Students who counsel with a professor who is striving to keep the commandments of God will be enriched and strengthened from the engagement. Students who study with faculty members who are loyal to the Church and its leaders, who are earnestly seeking to put first in their lives the things of God's kingdom, will come away from the BYU experience with an informed perspective that will tower above that which they might have received elsewhere.

In short, the quest for personal and institutional spirituality must underlie all we do.

The Prophet Joseph Smith explained, "It was my endeavor to so organize the Church, that the brethren [and sisters] might eventually be independent of every incumbrance beneath the celestial kingdom, by bonds and covenants of mutual friendship, and mutual love."[8] Elder Dallin H. Oaks declared to BYU students, "Love and tolerance are pluralistic, and that is their strength, but it is also the source of their potential weakness. Love and tolerance are incomplete *unless they are accompanied* by a concern for truth and a commitment to the unity God has commanded of his servants. Carried to an undisciplined excess, love and tolerance can produce indifference to truth and justice and opposition to unity. . . . The test of whether we are the Lord's is not just love and tolerance, *but unity*."[9]

President Brigham Young explained that "if this people would live their religion, and continue year after year to live their religion, it would not be many years before we should see eye to eye; . . . and the veil that now hangs over our minds would become so thin that we would actually see and discern things as they are."[10] "We are seeking to establish a oneness," Elder John Taylor observed,

> under the guidance and direction of the Almighty. . . . If there is any principle for which we contend with greater tenacity than another, it is this oneness. . . . To the world this principle is a gross error, for amongst them it is every man for himself; every man follows his own ideas, his own religion, his own morals, and the course in everything that suits his own notions. But the Lord dictates differently. We are under his guidance, and we should seek to be one with him and with all the authorities of His Church and kingdom on the earth in all the affairs of life. . . . This is what we are after, and when we have attained to this ourselves, we want to teach the nations of the earth the same pure principles that have emanated from the great Eloheim. We

want Zion to rise and shine that the glory of God may be manifest in her midst. . . . We never intend to stop until this point is attained through the teaching and guidance of the Lord and our obedience to His laws. Then, when men say unto us, "you are not like us," we reply, "we know it; we do not want to be. We want to be like the Lord, we want to secure His favor and approbation and to live under His smile, and to acknowledge, as ancient Israel did on a certain occasion, 'The Lord is our God, our judge, and our king, and He shall reign over us.'"[11]

We must have courage, the moral courage to stand up for what makes Brigham Young University distinctive, the moral courage to put down all that seeks to erode or hack away at that distinctiveness. This may prove to be a painful process. But there is a greater pain, the pain associated with knowing that we could have contributed to the realization of prophetic dreams concerning this place but chose to wait out the storm instead, only to find after the storm that we had lost something that cannot be retrieved. It is the pain known only to those who might have but did not.

Viewing all things through the lenses of the Restoration will then follow naturally and be reflected in the teachings and writings of men and women with regenerate hearts. And as we begin to do what we alone have been charged to do here at Brigham Young University, we will become a light to the religious and academic world; such will come, ironically, because we sought first the glory of God (see Matthew 6:33). In other words, if BYU is ever to achieve its prophetic destiny, is ever to make its mark in the world as a spiritual and intellectual Mount Everest, it must more closely approximate Mount Zion. As time passes, as President Spencer W. Kimball prophesied, there will be "a widening gap between this university and other universities both in terms of purposes and in terms of directions."[12]

THE BEST OF ALL WORLDS

I suppose I am suggesting that Brigham Young University is in fact "the best of all worlds," to borrow a phrase from Voltaire. It is an institution that is much more concerned with eternal discovery and spiritual certainty than with anything else. It is the best of all worlds in that it is a product of sacred sacrifice, an enterprise sustained by the tithes and prayers of Latter-day Saints all over the globe. It is the best of all worlds because it contains, as an article of its mission statement, the bold and distinctive declaration that it exists principally to assist individuals in their quest to obtain eternal life. It encourages character first and promotes personal integrity above all things, because its faculty and staff care even more about the spiritual growth and maturity of the students than we care about their intellectual growth (in fact, we care very much about both). It is the best of all worlds because we believe in the Almighty God, acknowledge him as our Father in Heaven, confess freely and unashamedly that Jesus of Nazareth was and is the Savior and Redeemer of humankind, and are poignantly aware that the clarity of our teaching and the success attending our research will depend largely upon our personal purity and our loyalty to true principles and true prophets.

BYU is the best of all worlds also because we have a perspective and a worldview that does not allow for a complete separation of the temporal and the spiritual. In a revelation given to the Prophet Joseph Smith in September 1830, the Savior declared that "all things unto me are spiritual, and not at any time have I given unto you a law which was temporal" (D&C 29:34). At the same time, we understand that the means, the methods for learning facts and uncovering truth may differ. On the relationship between our rational faculties, the power of reason, and our spiritual capacities, the place of revelation, Elder Oaks has written, "Reason is a thinking process using facts and logic that can be communicated to another person and tested by objective (that is, measurable) criteria. Revelation is communication from God to man. It cannot be defined and tested like reason. Reason involves thinking and demonstrating. Revelation involves hearing or seeing or understanding or feeling. Reason is potentially public. Revelation is invariably personal." Then, in stressing the innate limitations upon reason, he continued, "Despite the importance of study and reason, if we seek to learn of the things of God solely by this method, we are certain to stop short of our goal. We may even wind up at the wrong destination. Why is this so? On this subject God has prescribed the primacy of another method. To learn the things of God, what we need is not more study and reason, not more scholarship and technology, but more faith and revelation."[13]

Now to be sure, revelation for us does not represent a mystical distancing of one from reality, a transcendental separation of one's reason from the receipt of a revelation. The will of God is meant to be understood and to be as satisfying to the mind as it is to the heart. We are never instructed to give ourselves wholly to feelings any more than we are instructed to surrender all thought. In a revelation given to Joseph Smith and Oliver Cowdery in April 1829, we find these words: "Yea, behold, I will tell you in your mind and in your heart, by the Holy Ghost, which shall come upon you and which shall dwell in your heart" (D&C 8:2). My colleague Joseph McConkie has commented on this passage:

> We observe that neither [Oliver] nor Joseph was to experience any suspension of their natural faculties in the process of obtaining revelation. Quite to the contrary, their hearts and minds were to be the very media through which the revelation came. Prophets are not hollow shells through which the voice of the Lord echoes, nor are they mechanical recording devices; prophets are men of passion, feeling, intellect. One does not suspend agency, mind, or spirit in the service of God. It is . . . with heart, might, mind and strength that we have been asked to serve, and in nothing is this more apparent than the receiving of revelation. There is no mindless worship or service in the kingdom of heaven.[14]

RECONCILIATION AND RESPECT

During the last decade, I have been immersed thoroughly in the work of religious outreach and interfaith relations. I have spent hundreds if not thousands of hours seeking to understand and be understood. It has been a taxing labor, one that indeed has stretched my soul and expanded my intellect. There have been setbacks, to be sure, in the form of misunderstanding on the part of our respective religious constituencies, in the form of collegial misunderstanding and suspicion that I was giving away the store or compromising our distinctive doctrine. Most people who have drawn this conclusion—a faulty one, to be sure—have done so under the impression that significant progress cannot be made between otherwise warring religious factions unless someone compromises or concedes. I have come to know for myself, and have had it reinforced again and again, that this is not the case, that "convicted civility"[15] between persons of differing traditions can exist if we learn how to listen respectfully, be open to the mind-boggling idea that we can actually learn something from another who has differences, and be more concerned with winning a friend than winning an argument. When relationships of trust and respect and love are in place, doors open, knowledge flows, and the Spirit of the Lord works wonders. The Prince of Peace explained, "Where two or three are gathered together in my name, there am I in the midst of them" (Matthew 18:20).

If my Latter-day Saint colleagues and I can enjoy such a sweet brotherhood and sisterhood with a growing number of Evangelical Christians—a group with whom we have been in intense dialogue since 2000—then surely it is possible for men and women of faith who labor in varying avenues of science to enjoy cordial and collegial relationships with those involved in the study and teaching of religion, especially at Brigham Young University, the best of all worlds. Our epistemological thrusts may be different. Our presuppositions may be different. Our tests of validity and reliability may be different. But our hearts can be united as we strive to look beyond the dimensions of our disciplines toward higher goals. Some things we may and should reconcile here and now, while other matters may await further light and truth and additional discovery. "With an increasing body of facts," Elder John A. Widtsoe observed,

> there must needs be a constant demand for reconciliation among old and new conclusions. Such reconciliation should not be difficult, since all proper human activities aim to secure truth. Every person of honest mind loves truth above all else. In the proposed exchange of the new for the old, religion has often been in apparent conflict with science. Yet, the conflict has only been apparent, for science seeks truth, and the aim of religion is truth. That they have occupied different fields of truth is a mere detail. The gospel accepts and embraces all truth; science is slowly expanding her arms, and reaching into the invisible domain, in search of truth. The two are meeting daily. . . . Earnest attempts at reconciliation are rewarded with full success. Occasional failures are usually due to the mistake of alone trying religion. . . . Religion has an equal right to try science. Either method, properly applied, leads to the same result: truth is truth.[16]

THE DISCIPLINE OF FAITH

Faith has its own type of discipline. Some things that are obvious to the faithful sound like the gibberish of alien tongues to the faithless. The discipline of faith, the concentrated and consecrated effort to become single to God, has its own reward. It is worth considering the words of a revelation given in Kirtland, Ohio. The early Saints were told, "And as all have not faith, seek ye diligently and teach one another words of wisdom; . . . seek learning, even by study and also by faith" (D&C 88:118). We note that the counsel to seek learning out of the best books is prefaced by the negative clause, "And as all *have not* faith." One wonders whether what was not intended was something like the following: Since all do not have sufficient faith—have not "matured in their religious convictions" to learn by any other means[17]—then they must seek learning by study, through the use of the rational processes. Perhaps learning by studying from the best books would then be greatly enhanced by revelation. Honest truth seekers will learn things in this way that they could not know otherwise. This may be what Joseph Smith meant when he taught that "the best way to obtain truth and wisdom is not to ask it from books, but to go to God in prayer, and obtain divine teaching."[18] It is surely in this same context that another of the Prophet's famous yet little-understood statements finds meaning. "Could you gaze into heaven five minutes," he declared, "you would know more than you would by reading all that ever was written on the subject" of life after death.[19] "I believe in study," President Marion G. Romney stated. "I believe that men learn much through study. As a matter of fact, it has been my observation that they learn little concerning things as they are, as they were, or as they are to come without study. I also believe, however, and know, that learning by study is greatly accelerated by faith."[20]

President Harold B. Lee expressed the following to Brigham Young University students just weeks before his death in 1973: "'The acquiring of knowledge by faith is no easy road to learning. It will demand strenuous effort and continual striving by faith. In short, learning by faith is no task for a lazy man.' Someone has said, in effect, that 'such a process requires the bending of the whole soul, the calling up from the depths of the human mind and linking the person with God. The right connection must be formed; then only comes knowledge by faith, a kind of knowledge that goes beyond secular learning, that reaches into the realms of the unknown and makes those who follow that course great in the sight of the Lord.'"[21] On another occasion, President Lee taught that "learning by faith requires *the bending of the whole soul* through worthy living to become attuned to the Holy Spirit of the Lord, the calling up from the depths of one's own mental searching, and the linking of our own efforts to receive the true witness of the Spirit."[22]

No matter what our academic discipline, it is vital that we maintain our allegiance to the kingdom of God and never allow our discipline to dilute our discipleship. I made a decision many years ago that as a Latter-day Saint I was in this for the long haul and would never allow my faith to be held hostage by what had or had not been discovered or confirmed by external evidence. A while ago I spoke with an associate of another faith. I asked him what he thought of the recent claims by some to have located the very tomb and bones of Jesus Christ. To my surprise, he expressed serious concern. Almost jokingly I followed up: "Well, what would you do if it *was* proven beyond all doubt [which I rather think is utterly impossible] that those bones are indeed the very bones of Jesus of Nazareth?" He paused for a moment, reflected carefully, and said: "I guess I would have to denounce Christianity." "You must be kidding?" I fired back. "No," he said, "I take evidence very seriously." My last question, one that went unanswered, was, "And what about the evidence that lies deep within your soul, the evidence that burns within your bosom, the God-given assurance that Jesus lived, taught, performed miracles, suffered and died for us, and rose from the tomb in glorious immortality? What of that evidence?"

Elder Neal A. Maxwell has written, "It is [my] opinion that all the scriptures, including the Book of Mormon, will remain in the realm of faith. Science will not be able to prove or disprove holy writ. However, enough plausible evidence will come forth to prevent scoffers from having a field day, but not enough to remove the requirement of faith. Believers must be patient during such unfolding."[23]

Hugh Nibley, one of the great defenders of the faith, stated:

> The words of the prophets cannot be held to the tentative and defective tests that men have devised for them. Science, philosophy, and common sense all have a right to their day in court. But the last word does not lie with them. Every time men in their wisdom have come forth with the last word, other words have promptly followed. The last

word is a testimony of the gospel that comes only by direct revelation. Our Father in heaven speaks it, and if it were in perfect agreement with the science of today, it would surely be out of line with the science of tomorrow. Let us not, therefore, seek to hold God to the learned opinions of the moment when he speaks the language of eternity.[24]

I have learned a few things over the years. I thank God for the formal education I have received, for the privilege it is (and I count it such) to have received university training and to have earned bachelor's, master's, and doctoral degrees. Education has expanded my mind and opened conversations and doors for me. It has taught me what books to read, how to research a topic, and how to make my case or present my point of view more effectively. But the more I learn, the more I value the truths of salvation, those simple but profound verities that soothe and settle and sanctify human hearts.

I appreciate knowing that the order of the cosmos points toward a providential hand; I am deeply grateful to know, by the power of the Holy Ghost, that there is a God and that he is our Father in Heaven. I appreciate knowing something about the social, political, and religious world into which Jesus of Nazareth was born; I am deeply grateful for the witness of the Spirit that he is indeed God's Almighty Son.

I appreciate knowing something about the social and intellectual climate of nineteenth-century America; I am grateful to have a living witness that the Father and the Son appeared to Joseph Smith in the spring of 1820 and that what followed that theophany has been of God. In short, the more I encounter men's approximations to what is, the more I treasure those absolute truths that make known "things as they really are, and . . . things as they really will be" (Jacob 4:13; compare D&C 93:24). In fact, the more we learn, the more we begin to realize what we do not know, the more we feel the need to consider ourselves "fools before God" (2 Nephi 9:42).

CONCLUSION

When I think about all that has been done on this campus over the decades—about the prayers of dedication offered, the sermons preached, the thousands upon thousands of students prepared for meaningful service in a world that desperately needs them, and the fact that apostles and prophets have walked and talked and taught here—I want to quote the words of the Lord to Moses: "Put off thy shoes from off thy feet, for the place whereon thou standest is holy ground" (Exodus 3:5). There are things we are able to do here that are neither permitted nor comprehended elsewhere. If we as a community are willing to work with single-minded dedication to bring to pass God's righteousness, we will indeed become "a chosen generation, a royal priesthood, an holy nation, a peculiar people" who "shew forth the praises of him who hath called [us] out of darkness into his marvellous light" (1 Peter 2:9). The God of our fathers has his eye on this campus. This I know.

Thirty-four years ago I sat in the Smith Family Living Center wondering whether anything of worth would ever materialize in my life. I had completed both bachelor's and master's degrees in psychology here at BYU, had been accepted into a PhD program in clinical psychology, and, for all intents and purposes, everything should have been fine. There was only one major problem—I was not happy. I did not feel that I should continue my work in psychology, and in general I was wrestling with what I wanted to be when I grew up. One young faculty member, sensing my frustration and having desires akin to mine, sat and talked with me for over two hours. He read a statement by Charles H. Malik, former president of the United Nations General Assembly, a pronouncement that seems to me more prophetic as the years go by. "One day a great university will arise somewhere—I hope in America—to which Christ will return in His full glory and power, a university which will, in the promotion of scientific, intellectual, and artistic excellence, surpass by far even the best secular universities of the present, but which will at the same time enable Christ to bless it and act and feel perfectly at home in it."[25]

I felt the spirit of those words in 1973, and they brought hope and comfort to my heart; I still feel them as poignantly now. Such things will indeed come to pass. They will come to pass because men and women fully committed to the gospel of Jesus Christ—students, faculty, and staff—will take a leap of faith, will walk a few steps ahead of the light, and maybe even a bit into the darkness. Then will shine forth that kindly light amidst the encircling gloom in the world,[26] and Brigham Young University will have become a city on a hill. That we may properly prepare for our date with destiny is my prayer.

NOTES

1. Rodney J. Brown, "A Scientist's View of Life from a 'Mormon' Perspective," *Fundamentals of Life*, ed. Gyula Palyi, Claudia Zucchi, and Luciano Caglioti (New York: Elsevier, 2002), 518.
2. Søren Kierkegaard, *Purity of Heart Is to Will One Thing* (New York: Harper, 1956).
3. Elder Bruce R. McConkie has suggested that the power of God, the Light of Christ, faith, and priesthood power may well be the very same power. See *A New Witness for the Articles of Faith* (Salt Lake City: Deseret Book, 1985), 257.
4. Brown, "A Scientist's View," 519.
5. Arthur Holmes, *The Idea of a Christian College* (Grand Rapids, MI: Eerdmans, 1987), 5, 9.
6. Holmes, *Idea of a Christian College*, 7.
7. Marion G. Romney, "Temples of Learning," BYU Annual University Conference, September 1966.
8. Joseph Smith, *History of the Church of Jesus Christ of Latter-day Saints*, ed. B. H. Roberts, 2nd ed. rev. (Salt Lake City: Deseret Book, 1957), 1:269.
9. Dallin H. Oaks, "Our Strengths Can Become Our Downfall," in *1991–92 BYU Speeches of the Year* (Provo, UT: BYU Publications, 1992), 114; emphasis added.
10. Brigham Young, in *Journal of Discourses* (Liverpool: F. D. Richards, 1851–86), 3:194.

11. John Taylor, in *Journal of Discourses*, 11:346–47; emphasis added.
12. Spencer W. Kimball, *The Second Century of Brigham University* (Provo, UT: BYU Publications, 1975), 4.
13. Dallin H. Oaks, *The Lord's Way* (Salt Lake City: Deseret Book, 1991), 16–17, 19.
14. "The Principle of Revelation," in *Studies in Scripture*, vol. 1: *The Doctrine and Covenants*, ed. Robert L. Millet and Kent P. Jackson (Salt Lake City: Deseret Book, 1989), 83.
15. This term was coined by my evangelical Christian friend Richard J. Mouw in *Uncommon Decency: Christian Civility in an Uncivil World* (Downers Grove, IL: InterVarsity Press, 1992).
16. John A. Widtsoe, *In Search of Truth: Comments on the Gospel and Modern Thought* (Salt Lake City: Deseret Book, 1963), 15–16.
17. B. H. Roberts, quoted by Harold B. Lee, in Conference Report, April 1968, 129.
18. *Teachings of the Prophet Joseph Smith*, comp. Joseph Fielding Smith (Salt Lake City: Deseret Book, 1938), 191.
19. *Teachings of the Prophet Joseph Smith*, 324.
20. Marion G. Romney, *Learning for the Eternities* (Salt Lake City: Deseret Book, 1977), 72; emphasis added.
21. Harold B. Lee, "Be Loyal to the Royal Within You," in *1973 BYU Speeches of the Year* (Provo, UT: BYU Publications, 1974), 91.
22. Harold B. Lee, in Conference Report, April 1971, 94; emphasis added.
23. Neal A. Maxwell, *Plain and Precious Things* (Salt Lake City: Deseret Book, 1983), 4.
24. Hugh Nibley, *The World and the Prophets* (Salt Lake City: Deseret Book; Provo, UT: FARMS, 1987), 134.
25. Charles H. Malik, "Education and Upheaval: The Christian's Responsibility," *Creative Help for Daily Living* 21 (September 1970): 10.
26. See Boyd K. Packer, *The Holy Temple* (Salt Lake City: Bookcraft, 1980), 184.

J. Ward Moody

TIME IN SCRIPTURE AND SCIENCE: A CONCILIATORY KEY?

> Time is a sacred thing; it flows from heaven. . . . It is an emanation from that place whence eternity Springs. . . . It hath some assimilation to divinity.
> —Juan Eusebio Nieremberg[1]

OCCASIONALLY, WHEN DISCUSSING TEACHINGS FROM science and religion and how they mesh together, questions are posed that highlight apparent conflict between them. Three such questions are

1. What is the age of the earth? Is it seven days, 4.6 billion years, or something else entirely?
2. If death came with Adam some seven thousand years ago, how do we account for fossils?
3. Were Adam and Eve's bodies created miraculously in an instant, or was their creation an evolution over hundreds of millions of years?

And there are other questions that neither science nor religion satisfactorily answer. Two of these are

---

J. Ward Moody is a professor of physics and astronomy at Brigham Young University.

4. When did time begin? Was there a start, or has it always existed?
5. How will the universe end, or will it continue forever?

These are interesting questions chosen because of a common theme: they arise because we do not know what time is and how it can or cannot behave.

Time is a broad topic, and questions regarding it often ask different things. Question 1 on the age of the earth asks how long something has endured in time. Question 2 on Adam, death, and fossils deals not with endurance but asks which of several events came first. Question 3 on when Adam and Eve were created asks how the rather short duration of history since Genesis squares with the much longer time frame offered by the fossil record. It also asks if a creation event is to be understood as an instantaneous or gradual act. And questions 4 and 5 ask what time itself is and how or whether it can spring into being or blink out of existence.

To seek the answers to these questions, it is wise to first pursue a better understanding of the nature of time itself. Therefore, I first present some basic reasoning about time. I lay out what philosophers have said about its nature and, where possible, give an opinion on which thinking makes the most sense. And I point out ways that modern ideas of time allow some seemingly disparate views of science and religion to coexist harmoniously.

WHAT IS TIME?

First, what is time? Isaac Barrow, a mathematician at Cambridge and a mentor to Isaac Newton, wrote, "Because Mathematicians frequently make use of Time they ought to have a distinct idea of the meaning of that Word. Otherwise they are Quacks."[2] Thus warned, let me first tackle definitions. But this is not easy. The great fourth-century Catholic philosopher St. Augustine wrote, "For what is time? Who can easily and briefly explain it? Who can even comprehend it in thought or put the answer into words? Yet is it not true that in conversation we refer to nothing more familiarly or knowingly than time? And surely we understand it when we speak of it; we understand it also when we hear another speak of it. What, then, is time? If no one asks me, I know what it is. If I wish to explain it to him who asks me, I do not know."[3]

St. Augustine's humble humor is delightful as well as insightful. With tongue in cheek, I offer these statements: "Time is what keeps everything from happening at once," and "Time is just one darn thing after another." Besides being jokes, both are actually decent philosophical statements. The first says that time imposes structure and order. It is a space that helps organize the things within it. The second is a different approach. It says time is not a space that forces organization, it is the organization itself—the sequencing of events. To be honest, these two statements are as profound as some of the thinking gets.

The temporal philosopher Huw Price remarked, "The philosophy of time has a long history, and is unusual even by philosophical standards for the durability of some of its main concerns. In a modern translation much of St. Augustine's work on time would pass for twentieth-century philosophy."[4] St. Augustine feared not to delve into esoteric topics. His writings on time are incisive and profound. In his temporal musings, he puzzled at length on many issues, but two deserve our attention here. One was the distinction between the past, the present, and the future. The past and the future to him seem unreal. The past has ceased to exist, and the future does not yet exist. And yet the present moment is determined by the past, and the future is determined by the present. So in some sense, past, present, and future must be real and must be interconnected. The second puzzle was about the apparent flow of time and why it should compel us forward, as it were, into new temporal spaces. Price puts it this way:

> Two problems—[the past-present-future distinction and the flow of time]—remain the focus of much work in the philosophy of time. . . . Philosophers tend to divide into

two camps. On one side are those who regard the passage of time as an objective feature of reality and interpret the present moment as the marker or leading edge of this advance. Some members of this camp [share] Augustine's view that the past and future are unreal. Others take the view that the past is real in a way that the future is not so that the present consists in something like coming into being of determinate reality.[5]

I would enlarge upon this idea and assert that the division into camps can be reduced to asking if time is a *space* or *dimension* in its own right, or if it is a *journey through space*. Make that distinction, and from there different possibilities unfold.

TIME AS A SPACE

Treat time as a space, and the present becomes a subjective notion. *Now* is dependent on one's viewpoint in much the same way that *here* is. In this view, there is no objective division of the world into the past, present, and future, just as there is no objective division of space into *here* and *there*. Such a view can lead to the conclusion that there is no significant difference between the past, present, and future.

It is tempting to stop and shout, "Of course there is a difference! The past is behind, the future is ahead and the present is now! Only dimwitted philosophers could get confused about such an obvious thing!" Indeed! But there *are* some physical, philosophical, and religious facts that challenge such a straightforward interpretation.

When Albert Einstein gave the world the special theory of relativity, he irrefutably established that events which are simultaneous to one person are not simultaneous to another person moving with respect to the first. To illustrate, suppose someone on Earth experiences two events at the exact same time. Call the moment these events occur "now." Someone moving rapidly past Earth would not see these events taking place at a single specific time. For this traveler, the event times will separate more and more with increasing speed until at the speed of light one event happens instantaneously and the other event is infinitely distant in the future. If this person were traveling at the speed of light when time began, then we can say their existence between those events—which now stretches from the beginning of time to the infinite future—will be played out in what is perceived to be a single instant on Earth.[6] Taken to the extreme, if time is a space, we can argue that there exists an infinitely large set of perspectives, defined by all possible velocities and locations, that eternally experiences every point in time as being now. So a person's location in time can be different depending on his or her relative speeds, and it is philosophically possible to assign every instant of time as being "now" to someone. Therefore "now" is not unique, and thus neither are the past and future.

Leaving physics and relativity for a minute and turning to religion, let us enlarge the concept of "now" to be a single day. A day is twenty-four hours long, but when considering a universe that is billions of years old, a day is like an instant. So rename "now" as "today." Consider, then, these scriptures and how they refer to "today":

> Hear my voice *while it is called today*, and harden not your hearts. (D&C 45:6; emphasis added).

> Behold, *now it is called today* until the coming of the Son of Man, and verily it is a day of sacrifice, and a day for the tithing of my people; for he that is tithed shall not be burned at his coming.
> For after today cometh the burning—this is speaking after the manner of the Lord—for verily I say tomorrow all the proud and they that do wickedly shall be as stubble....
> Wherefore if ye believe me, ye will labor *while it is called today*. (D&C 64:23–25; emphasis added)

The phraseology is curious. In the expression "while it is called today," "it" sounds like an entity that we on Earth simply refer to as "today"; one can imagine that God, on the other hand, may refer to or experience "it" differently. Perhaps God is subtly telling us that our "now" of "today" is not something that he experiences in the same way. If so, this is consistent with the notion that "now" is not the same everywhere in the universe.

There is an interesting conclusion possible from this manner of thinking. If every point of time can be called "now" according to some perspective, then the entire extent of time must already be created. You cannot say that, at this instant, a point of time is known to be "now" before it has come into being. Therefore all time—and with it, all past, present, and future—must already exist. If so, it is trivial for God to know the future.

The notion that the past, present, and future already exist is sometimes referred to as "block time"—time being a block of space that different people may move through differently. There are some philosophical problems with it. First, not all positions and speeds are actually realized. That is, there is not some entity located at all points in space that is moving with all possible velocities. Therefore, there is nothing physical forcing all the "nows" to be real. Second, when people interact with each other, they are always at the same location in time. So even if they can occupy different "nows" under different circumstances, there is no immediate interaction between these different "nows," making their distinction less significant.

Even though block time allows for God to comprehend all time, I am uncomfortable with it from a religious perspective. It seems a bit like predestination, with our decisions already made and existing in a future that can only unfold to us as our "now" hyperplane passes through it. I see no purpose in living in such a universe. If I know anything about life from my own experience, it is that we have agency. Our decisions matter and are not made before we make them.[7] Time must allow for this.

TIME AS A JOURNEY

Now consider time not as a space itself but rather as the marking of a journey through space. With this approach, the past is more readily separated from the future. The past is where you have been, and the future is where you will go. We exist on the thin membrane of "now," plodding along with it into the future.

The moving slice of time in which we dwell is reality. Kurt Gödel, a Nobel Prize–winning mathematician and philosopher who thought a lot about time and reality, made this statement: "Reality consists of an infinity of layers of 'now' which come into existence successively."[8] And the great philosopher René Descartes believed that "a material body has the property of spatial extension but no inherent capacity for temporal endurance and that God by his continual action recreates the body at each successive instant."[9] Time, therefore, is a divine process of re-creation. These points of view assert that once a moment has passed, so has the reality that experienced the moment. Therefore, Descartes suggests, God has to re-create reality for it to persist. This would be a constant act like Atlas holding up the sky. Indeed, it is hard to see how there would be room in God's schedule to do anything beside the drudgery of eternally recreating "now." Of course, one can disagree with Descartes and equally well assert that the material objects occupying "now" keep their reality and simply ride along with time.

The current moment is vanishingly small. One can argue that if reality only exists in a time space that is infinitesimally short, it does not exist at all. Fortunately, mathematics has already tackled the notion of a vanishingly small interval with the derivative. Derivatives are real and are the foundation of calculus. In a sense, "now" is like a derivative—the instantaneous snapshot of a smoothly evolving journey. Puzzling over time's "fleeting moment" illustrates how hard it is to comprehend a derivative. (But it does make for an occasional nice poem!)

Regardless of other ramifications, one *can* take the view that "now" is the only thing that exists. The past behind us has gone out of existence. The future does not yet exist. Time functions as the process of continually re-creating "now," shunting the future to the past. Call this point of view "now only."

How we get from the past to the future is guided by a concept called "causality." Causality says that the cause of an effect must precede the effect in time and thus gives a unique order to "causally connected events." That is, throw a rock at a window, and the window will not break before the rock hits it. Therefore, from all perspectives that can exist, the act of the rock being thrown will precede the breaking it caused. In this approach, time is the connection between actions. The moment of the connection is "now." At this moment a unique reality emerges from all the potential realities that might be.[10]

Now we come to two alternatives. Once a moment has gone into the past, it may or may not be real in the sense that it physically exists. Something that is real can be visited, at least in principle. If you somehow had the means, you could go to the place where it resides and find it. But if it is not real, then it either never existed or in this case has ceased to exist; nowhere in the universe can you go and find it. A past that is no longer real is consistent with "now only."

The other approach I will call "unfolding time." This says that time is the "leading edge" of a space whose past is made real by the passage of time. The past is real, but the future is not. This contrasts with block time, in which both future and past are real and partitioned only by the moving membrane of time. So we have three possibilities covered: "Now only" says that only the present is real. "Unfolding time" says that the present and past are real but the future is not. "Block time" says that past, present, and future are all real. There are arguments in science supporting all three positions.

Turning thoughts to religion, again consider Doctrine and Covenants 45:6 and 64:23–25. The special significance of "it" being called "today" can also point to "now" being the salient part of what time is. "It" then becomes time itself, and "today" is the only part of it that is real—at least to us. We must do actions *now* for them to be *real*.

I am inclined to accept time as the leading edge that creates a real past out of an indeterminate future as suggested by unfolding time. Reality is the place currently occupied by now. Our past actions are made real by time and, being real, are something for which we are accountable to God. But I must confess that even though this appeals to me, I have no idea how a person could ever go back and visit the past. So perhaps "now only" has the greater argument and our past actions are real only for how they affect us and others now.

TIME AND MOTION

Time may be a space, or it may be a journey. Either way, it is connected with how things change in the universe. This, in turn, means it is inextricably connected with motion, for change always involves motion. Bas C. Van Fraassen wrote, "Time is neither identical with nor entirely independent of movement, and it remains for us to determine the relation between them."[11] To illustrate this important point, think of an example of time passing—a clock ticking, the sun rising and setting, commuting to work, and so on. Can you come up with an example where you can say, "OK, in this situation time passed, but there was no motion involved"? You might say, "I am going to sit motionless in a room, and I am going to do it for one minute." So you sit there motionless and nothing changed in that room, right? Not quite. We measure time with ticks of a clock. If you did not have a clock and had not seen the seconds count to sixty, you would not have known you were there for a minute. So the passage of time is known from the motion inside the clock.

How about traveling? On a family vacation, were you ever guilty of pestering your folks with "Are we there yet? Are we there yet?" as time seemed to crawl? If you have a steady velocity and you know the distance to your destination, then the time to take the trip is well determined. Taking a trip is a supreme example of marking time with motion.

How about growing older? If a person ages, where is the motion there? This is more subtle, but aging involves changes in our bodies, changes that come about because of molecular movements. Living, breathing, walking, talking, even the act of thinking involves movement on the molecular level.

I cannot think of a single example of time being proven to elapse without a reference to things moving. Henri Poincaré, a great physicist of the last century, took motion to be the defining nature of time and wrote, "Time should be so defined that the equations of mechanics may be as simple as possible."[12] That is a philosophical statement that serves us well—whatever the universe is or is not, it is simple. This notion, called Occam's razor, is one of the guiding principles of science. Leonhard Euler, a great mathematician and a decent person, enlarged upon Poincaré's idea with the assertion that time is properly defined when Newton's first law of motion holds true.[13]

The straightforward simplicity of Euler's idea makes it very solid. But not all agree. We go back to Isaac Barrow: "But does not time imply motion? Not at all, I reply, as far as its absolute, intrinsic nature is concerned; no more than rest; the quality of time depends on neither essentially; whether things run or stand still, whether we sleep or wake, time flows in its even tenor. Imagine all the stars to have remained fixed from their birth; nothing would have been lost to time; as long would that stillness have endured as has continued the flow of this motion."[14] Barrow is pointing out that stars in space take fixed, well-defined times to move in their orbits. Imagine a formerly star-filled universe with the stars removed. Barrow says time would flow in that space just as surely and at the same rate as if the stars were present. We could not prove it—that is the problem—but he says it would be there regardless. Isaac Newton the student says, "Absolute, true, and mathematical time, of itself, and from its own nature, flows equably without relation to anything external, and by another name is called duration. . . . For times and spaces are, as it were, the places as well of themselves as of all other things."[15]

Regardless, most agree that time is connected to motion. Gottfried Leibniz expressed the thoughts of many when he wrote that for "a duration without changes, it would be impossible to determine its length."[16] Or in other words, time can only be defined when there are objects changing and we can measure the change. If nothing happens, no time elapses.

We know that God's motion is different from ours. Angels appear and disappear suddenly and otherwise come and go in ways we cannot come and go. If time and motion are connected, as most scientists believe, then it should be no surprise that God's time can be as different from our time as his motion is. It should therefore neither puzzle nor distress us to measure or infer time scales in science that are different from those in scripture.

THE FLOW OF TIME

Another aspect of time agreed upon by all points of view is that it advances. Newton reasonably argued that the rate of this advance is always the same. But this is not the modern view. C. S. Lewis touched upon time flowing at a different rate in *Perelandra*. Follow the conversation between his Eve, called the Green Lady, and his developing Christ figure, a traveler named Ransom:

> "I was young yesterday," she said. "When I laughed at you. Now I know that the people in your world do not like to be laughed at."
>
> "You say you were young?"
>
> "Yes."
>
> "Are you not young to-day also?"
>
> She appeared to be thinking for a few moments, so intently that the flowers dropped, unregarded, from her hand.
>
> "I see it now," she said presently. "It is very strange to say one is young at the moment one is speaking. But tomorrow I shall be older. And then I shall say I was young to-day. You are quite right. This is great wisdom you are bringing. . . ."
>
> "What do you mean?"

"This looking backward and forward along the line and seeing how a day has one appearance as it comes to you, and another when you are in it, and a third when it has gone past. Like the waves."

"But you are very little older than yesterday."

"How do you know that?"

"I mean," said Ransom, "a night is not a very long time."

She thought again, and then spoke suddenly, her face lightening. "I see it now," she said. "You think times have lengths. A night is always a night whatever you do in it, as from this tree to that is always so many paces whether you take them quickly or slowly. I suppose that is true in a way. But the waves do not always come at equal distances."[17]

And so the Green Lady learned from a rather one-sided conversation with Ransom. She gave him credit for enlightening her while stating the greater insight. "The waves do not always come at equal distances" means that time need not always flow at an equal rate.

C. S. Lewis is making the point, well understood in his time from the special and general theories of relativity, that time is not the rigid, steadily flowing entity Newton describes. Rather its flow can be different at different locations. A good example is a black hole, where time slows down for those who approach the event horizon. Another famous example from the special theory of relativity is the twin paradox, where two identical twins age differently depending on how they travel. Time flowing at different rates depending on location and acceleration has been embedded in mainstream physics since about the 1920s.

The gospel agrees with this. In the question and answer session that is Doctrine and Covenants 130, the Prophet Joseph Smith writes, "In answer to the question—Is not the reckoning of God's time, angel's time, prophet's time and man's time, according to the planet on which they reside? I answer, Yes. . . . [The angels] reside in the presence of God, on a globe like a sea of glass and fire, where all things for their glory are manifest, past, present, and future, and are continually before the Lord" (vv. 4–5, 7). Whatever else may be contained in these scriptures, they support the notion that time is different in different places. In Abraham 3:4 we read, "Kolob was after the manner of the Lord, according to its times and seasons in the revolutions thereof, that one revolution was a day unto the Lord, after his manner of reckoning, it being one thousand years according to the time appointed unto that whereon thou standest." The same idea is found in 2 Peter 3:8: "One day is with the Lord as a thousand years, and a thousand years as one day." I do not believe these passages need be interpreted as saying there is literally a calendar in Kolob that registers one thousand Earth years for every twenty-four-hour Kolobian day. Rather, I think the greater message is that for God time is not the same entity flowing in the same fashion that it does for us. As Alma the Younger states in Alma 40:8, "All is as one day with God, and time only is measured unto men."

TIME AS CHOICE

Simple interactions between moving bodies can alter their motion. How this motion is altered is derived from the laws of motion. These laws reveal how past motion has led to the present state, and how future motion will come from the present state. The laws of motion teach us that in any interaction, energy and momentum are conserved and are therefore the same after the interaction as they were before. Because total energy and momentum do not change with time we say that the equations of motion prefer no temporal direction.

But the science of thermodynamics discovered a unique principle called "the law of increasing disorder" that says the randomness or disorder of energy does change and increases with time. Several people, including the great astrophysicist Sir Arthur Eddington, have pointed out that this may be the only principle of nature that fundamentally prefers a direction of time. Eddington has suggested that time itself may be related to or defined by this law: "Let us draw an arrow arbitrarily. If as we follow the arrow we find more and more of the random element in the state of the world, then the arrow is pointing towards the future; if the random element decreases, the arrow points towards the past. . . . I shall use the phrase 'time's arrow' to express this one-way property of time which has no analogue in space."[18]

The concept of disorder can be illustrated by a bedroom. You yourself have to take the energy and the time to make sure things are hung up and put away neatly. If you do not expend the energy to carefully put things away, they end up in random places. Nature by itself will not hang up the clothes. In the same way, nature by itself will not create greater order in any process but will drive things to greater disorder with increasing time. Clothes will wear out, cars will break down, tree leaves will fall and decay. Things need to be repaired or replaced, using organized energy, to preserve the status quo or to improve things. When you think about it, much of what we do with our time and energy in this life is to counter the effects of this law.

Here is speculation that must be viewed as such. Adam and Eve lived in a garden where they did not have to farm to obtain food. The Garden of Eden took care of itself and brought forth fruit spontaneously without labor. Does this mean the law of increasing disorder was not in effect for them? After the Fall they were cast into a world where they earned their bread by the sweat of their brow, fighting, as we do today, the consequences of increasing disorder. Was the Fall of Adam an injection into a world where the law of increasing disorder, and hence time, functions as we know it now, while before in Eden it did not? Can we say, then, that time as we know it began at the Fall?

Alma the Younger, in reference to the Fall of Adam, wrote, "And thus we see, that there was a time granted unto man to repent, yea, a probationary time, a time to repent and serve God" (Alma 42:4). The Fall cast Adam and Eve into a world where they could choose for themselves. They could choose before then, but not in the same full sense that they could after the Fall. If time as we know it and choice as we know it both began at the Fall, then perhaps time as a series of events can be recast as time being a progressive series of choices or decisions. Time is what facilitates choice. We have been placed on this temporal earth to make choices. The march of time is going to make us choose no matter what. You chose to read this book. When you have finished reading you will choose to do something else. You do not have a choice about making choices: time is going to force you to make them.

Amulek says in Alma 34:32–33, "For behold, this life is the time for men to prepare to meet God; yea, behold the day of this life is the day for men to perform their labors. . . . For after this day of life, which is given us to prepare for eternity, behold, if we do not improve our time while in this life, then cometh the night of darkness wherein there can be no labor performed." There are certain actions we do here and certain choices we make. When we go to the next life, we do not act and choose in the same way we do now. God has already made the choices that brought him to his exalted station, so he does not now need to choose in the same sense that we choose. Therefore, it makes sense that his time is not our time in the same way that his choices are not on the same plane as our choices. Could this be part of what he is communicating when he says that time is only measured unto man?

THE BEGINNING OF TIME

In the twentieth century, astronomers and theoretical physicists concluded that the amount of past time is finite and thus there was a beginning to our universe. This beginning was a perfectly ordered, creative infusion of energy into space called the big bang. In the 1960s there was a competing theory, the steady state, which says the universe has always been and will always be in its current state. The steady state theory has been rejected in the face of overwhelming evidence of a creation that occurred about 13.7 billion years ago. Today only the big bang theory is considered viable by the vast majority of scientists.

Was the big bang the beginning of time as well? Was there no time anywhere, then suddenly there *was* time? To put it another way, was there a big bang button that existed somewhere that God *took the time* to push? Or did all existence, including that of God, begin at once in some defining event that heralded the beginning of all other events and thus the start of time itself?

How can time begin? How can there be nothing that suddenly becomes something? It makes no sense. But how can time *not* begin? Can it just go forever both to the past and future? This does not seem to make much sense either. But reject both possibilities and all that is left is a conundrum. Our mortal minds seem to have no capacity to comprehend even the *possible* answers to the question of time beginning.

In the King Follett Discourse, the Prophet Joseph taught, "Is it logical to say that a spirit is immortal and yet have a beginning? Because if a spirit of man had a beginning, it will have an end, *but it does not have a beginning or end.*"[19] Elsewhere in the same speech he declares matter to also be eternal, with neither beginning nor end. So if time equates with existence of matter and spirits, there was no beginning to time.

St. Augustine attempted a resolution to this question by postulating that God is "outside of time." Writing in *Confessions XI*, he states that time itself was part of God's creation. There was simply no before, and all who question what God was or what he was doing before time began are "still full of their old carnal nature."[20] The great cosmologist Stephen Hawking stated, "Hubble's observations suggested that there was a time, called the big bang, when the universe was infinitesimally small and infinitely dense. Under such conditions all the laws of science, and therefore all ability to predict the future, would break down. If there were events earlier than this time, then they could not affect what happens at the present time. Their existence can be ignored because it would have no observational consequences. One may say that time had a beginning at the big bang, in the sense that earlier times simply would not be defined."[21] Augustine and Hawking are saying essentially the same thing: before the creation of the universe, time as we know it had no meaning. It may have meaning to God, but it has no meaning for us.

Alan Guth is a theoretical physicist who came up with the idea of inflationary cosmology, a tenet of the big bang theory. Once, after presenting at a conference, he was asked, "What happened before the big bang?" Everyone snickered and wondered what he would say. We thought he would laugh back, but he did not. Instead he said rather soberly, "I think about that all the time. I do not know the answer but I keep thinking about it."[22] The Prophet Joseph Smith's firm declaration that matter and spirit have no beginning is as rational as any philosophy. My own feeling is that the big bang may have marked a beginning of time for our universe and was likely a momentous event of eternal significance. But it was not the beginning of God nor of existence itself.

THE END OF TIME

As a child in church, I heard a speaker give an analogy of eternity. Said he, "Consider a one-mile square granite block. Every year a sparrow comes and pecks at it once. Eternity is longer than the time it will take to erode the block to dust." That was a very effective analogy to a Valiant A. I must confess that I was so intrigued by it that I did the math and estimated it would be about 10^{21} seconds or thirty trillion years. That is a very long time, but it still has an end. Eternity has no end.

A good friend and scholar, David Derrick, once pointed out that when you have a limitless abundance of something, its value is impossible to appreciate. For example, if you have all the gold in the world, then what worth is gold? The story goes that there was a rich man who had lived a good life and wanted to take his wealth with him when he died. So he pleaded with the Lord, who finally said, "OK, we will liquidate your estate, turn it into gold, and deliver it to you in a suitcase at the pearly gates." When he died, sure enough, there was the suitcase filled with gold! St. Peter greeted him with "Welcome! You have lived a wonderful life. Come in!

Hey, what's in the suitcase?" The man opened it, and St. Peter exclaimed, "Oh, gold. That's nice. What did you want to bring street pavement for?"

Eternity is most often taught as being an infinite supply of time. Can you feel hurried to accomplish anything if you have an infinite amount of time to do it in? No—like infinite gold, it would be of small value. As David pointed out, our time is not infinite—we have deadlines, death being a particularly impressive one. God reminds us of them continually. He teaches us that they are important and that we should prepare for them. Is it possible that this life is the place where we learn for the first time what the "progression" of eternal progression is: change accomplished through actions which are urgent only because we have limited time in which to do them? Maybe one of the points of the Fall of Adam is the limited time. Maybe the stress of meeting deadlines is a great education on the blessing of time.

The big bang admits to no end of time. It speculates on different possible expansion rates and distributions of matter in the universe as it ages but assumes that the universe will continue forever without time reaching an end.

Scripture talks of eternity which has no end. Yet it also talks of an end to time. The interesting phrase "time no longer" comes up several times. Doctrine and Covenants 88:110 says, "And [the angel] shall stand forth upon the land and upon the sea, and swear in the name of him who sitteth upon the throne, that there shall be time no longer." If the definition of time spoken here is a space in which we act, then the end of time would mean the end of actions, which makes no sense. Actions clearly follow this: Satan is bound for a period of time and loosed for a season, there is battle, and so on. The Greek version of the book of Revelation speaks of the same events with words indicating that "time" means "no more delay."[23] That may be simply what it means—no more waiting around for the final acts to take place.

But if time means the ability to choose as we do now, then the end of time may refer to the end of the probationary period given to man that started at the Fall. It would not be the end of all actions but rather the end of the *kinds* of actions we do on this earth—the kinds that began when our probationary time started. If so, this supports God being outside the time of man, since he did not fall with Adam, and outside of the effects of the law of increasing disorder—my expansion to Eddington's idea. Spirit and matter would still be eternal, existing before Adam fell and before our clocks started ticking.

Well, it is great fun to think about these things. I hope there are some useful insights in here somewhere. I end my thoughts with St. Augustine's wonderful comment on those who speculate on the creation of time. Said he, "How, then, shall I respond to him who asks, 'What was God doing *before* he made heaven and earth?' I do not answer, as a certain one is reported to have done facetiously (shrugging off the force of the question). 'He was preparing hell,' he said, 'for those who pry too deep.' It is one thing to see the answer; it is another to laugh at the questioner—and for myself I do not answer these things thus. More willingly would I have answered, 'I do not know what I do not know,' than cause one who asked a deep question to be ridiculed—and by such tactics gain praise for a worthless answer."[24] With that, I need to thank you for, well, your time.

NOTES

1. *Of Temperance and Patience*, trans. Henry Vaughan, in *The Works in Verse and Prose Complete of Henry Vaughan, Silurist*, ed. Alexander B. Grosart (Lancashire, UK: n.p., 1871), 4:108; spelling modernized.
2. Isaac Barrow, quoted by Paul Davies, *About Time* (New York: Simon and Schuster, 1995), 183.
3. St. Augustine, *Confessions*, 11:17, in *Confessions and Enchiridion*, trans. and ed. Albert C. Outler, Christian Classics Ethereal Library, http://www.ccel.org/ccel/augustine/confessions.xiv.html.
4. Huw Price, *Time's Arrow and Archimedes' Point: New Directions for the Physics of Time* (New York: Oxford University Press, 1996), 12.
5. Price, *Time's Arrow*, 12.

6. There are exact requirements not fully explained for this to be true. The traveler must be moving toward the location of one event and away from the other. And they must be passing Earth when the person on Earth sees the two events occur simultaneously. These constraints, though, do not weaken the principle.
7. There is much in the science of quantum mechanics that supports this point of view. Unfortunately I do not have the time or expertise to present it here.
8. Kurt Gödel, "A Remark about the Relationship between Relativity Theory and Idealistic Philosophy," in *Albert Einstein: Philosopher-Scientist*, ed. P. A. Schilpp (La Salle, IL: Open Court, 1949), 557.
9. G. J. Whitrow, "The Laws of Motion," *British Journal for the History of Science* 5, no. 3 (June 1971): 226.
10. There are some who argue that causality is not necessary. See Julian Barbour's *The End of Time: The Next Revolution in Physics* (New York, Oxford University Press, 2001) for an interesting presentation of this odd point of view. I do not dwell on it because I consider it to be too unlikely.
11. Bas C. van Fraassen, *An Introduction to the Philosophy of Time and Space* (New York: Random House, 1970), 15.
12. Henri Poincaré, *The Foundations of Science*, trans. G. B. Halsted (New York: Science Press, 1913), 227–28.
13. Leonhard Euler, *Opera Omnia*, ed. F. Rudo and others, Series III (Berlin Teubner, 1911–67), 2:376–83.
14. *The Geometrical Lectures of Isaac Barrow*, trans. J. M. Child (La Salle, IL: Open Court, 1916), 35–37, quoted in van Fraassen, *Philosophy of Time and Space*, 22.
15. Isaac Newton, *Principia*, vol. 1, *The Motion of Bodies*, trans. Andrew Motte, rev. Florian Cajori (Berkeley: University of California Press, 1960), 6, 8.
16. Gottfried Leibniz, *New Essays Concerning Human Understanding*, trans. A. G. Langley (La Salle, IL: Open Court, 1916), book 2, section xv, 11.
17. C. S. Lewis, *Perelandra* (New York: Macmillan, 1965), 60.
18. Arthur Stanley Eddington, *The Nature of the Physical World* (New York: Cambridge University Press, 1929), 69.

19. Stan Larson, "The King Follett Discourse: A Newly Amalgamated Text," *BYU Studies* 18, no 2 (1978): 11. Italics are from this source and indicate words found only in the Wilford Woodruff manuscript.
20. Augustine, *Confessions*, 11:12.
21. Stephen W. Hawking, *A Brief History of Time: From the Big Bang to Black Holes* (New York: Bantam Books, 1988), 9.
22. Alan Guth, "Astrophysical Ages and Time Scales," lecture at Hilo, Hawaii, February 5–9, 2001.
23. Private communication with Michael D. Rhodes.
24. Augustine, *Confessions*, 11:14.

NASA, ESA, M. Robberto (STScI/ESA) and The Hubble Space Telescope Orion Treasury Project Team.

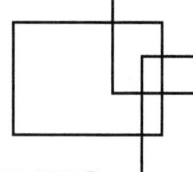

Michael D. Rhodes

The Scriptural Accounts of the Creation: A Scientific Perspective

THE PURPOSE OF THIS PAPER IS TO EXAMINE THE SCRIPtural accounts of the Creation from a scientific point of view with particular emphasis on physics and astronomy, although of necessity I will also have to deal to some extent with biology, chemistry, and geology. The views expressed here are my own and are not meant to represent the views of The Church of Jesus Christ of Latter-day Saints or Brigham Young University. They are a distillation of my thoughts and conclusions over two decades of teaching and research.

BASIC PRINCIPLES

As we deal with the Creation, I suggest that there are some basic principles that we need to follow in our quest for truth. Both science and religion have as a major purpose the search for truth. But what is truth? I believe that the best definition comes from the Doctrine and Covenants: "Truth is knowledge of things as they are, and as they were, and as they are to come" (93:24). Truth, then, is knowledge of things as they really are—past, present, and future. Although the methodology of science and religion differ, both are ways of learning about truth. Brigham Young stated, "The idea that the religion of Christ is one thing,

---

Michael D. Rhodes is an associate research professor of ancient scripture at Brigham Young University.

and science is another, is a mistaken idea, for there is no true religion without true science, and consequently there is no true science without true religion."[1] The emphasis, of course, must be on *true* science and *true* religion. When seeming conflicts arise, either the scientific principle is wrong or our understanding of the revealed religious concept is mistaken or incomplete. When discrepancies do arise, the revealed word of God must take precedence. As President Harold B. Lee said, "In all your learning, measure it and test it by the white light of truth revealed to the prophets of God and you will never be led astray."[2] We must, however, also be careful in our interpretation of revealed truth. We must not "wrest" the scriptures, as Peter warns (see 2 Peter 3:16), trying to draw conclusions from them that are not warranted. We need to develop a humble recognition of the limitations of our understanding of and our ability to interpret both scripture and science. Dogmatism, pride, and prejudice can cloud our judgment and mislead us.

Elder Bruce R. McConkie made a critically important observation: "Our knowledge about the creation is limited. We do not know the how and why and when of all things. Our finite limitations are such that we could not comprehend them if they were revealed to us in all their glory, fullness, and perfection. What has been revealed is that portion of the Lord's eternal word which we must believe and understand if we are to envision the truth about the Fall and the Atonement and thus become heirs of salvation."[3] Our knowledge, both scriptural and scientific, is limited. We need to keep that constantly in mind.

Elder James E. Talmage gave this vital insight:

> Discrepancies that trouble us now will diminish as our knowledge of pertinent facts is extended. The Creator has made a record in the rocks for man to decipher; but He has also spoken directly regarding the main stages of progress by which the earth has been brought to be what it is. The accounts cannot be fundamentally opposed; one cannot

The Scriptural Accounts of the Creation

contradict the other; though man's interpretation of either may be seriously at fault. . . .

Let us not try to wrest the scriptures in an attempt to explain away what we cannot explain. The opening chapters of *Genesis*, and scriptures related thereto, were never intended as a textbook of geology, archeology, earth-science or man-science. Holy Scripture will endure, while the conceptions of men change with new discoveries. We do not show reverence for the scriptures when we misapply them through faulty interpretation.[4]

We may become frustrated that the Lord has not revealed more to us—there are so many details we simply do not have any information on, but President Boyd K. Packer explains, "If all things were known, man's creativity would be stifled. There could be no further discovery, no growth, nothing to decide—no agency. All things not only *are not* known but *must not* be so convincingly clear as to eliminate the need for faith. That would nullify agency and defeat the purpose of the plan of salvation."[5] Because of our limited knowledge and understanding, differences of opinion will inevitably arise, but in the words of President Gordon B. Hinckley, "we can disagree without being disagreeable."[6]

For believing Latter-day Saints, another important concept is God's intimate involvement in the Creation. The scriptural accounts make it clear that the Creation was not simply a mechanistic unfolding of events driven by natural law. Each scriptural account shows God playing a direct, integral, and continuous part in the Creation; he did not just wind the clock at the beginning and then stand back and let things develop on their own. Abraham's account of the Creation is perhaps clearest in emphasizing this. For example:

> And then the Lord said: Let us go down. And they went down at the beginning, and they, that is the Gods, organized and formed the heavens and the earth. . . .

> And the Gods ordered, saying: Let the waters under the heaven be gathered together unto one place, and let the earth come up dry. . . .
> And the Gods saw that they were obeyed. . . .
> And the Gods watched those things which they had ordered until they obeyed. . . .
> And the Gods said: Let us prepare the waters to bring forth abundantly the moving creatures that have life. . . .
> And the Gods saw that they would be obeyed. . . .
> And the Gods prepared the earth to bring forth the living creature after his kind. (4:1, 4–5, 9–10, 18, 21, 24)

All these passages indicate that God was carefully involved in all aspects of the Creation, observing what took place and intervening to ensure that all things worked out in accordance with his plan.

Elder McConkie emphasized this point:

> All created things, this earth and all that is thereon—all things were and are made, not by man's power, not by some undirected forces of nature or of the universe. There was no happenstance in creation, no chance creation of life in the primordial swamps, on development up from one species to another by evolutionary processes. The creation was planned, organized, and controlled. It came by God's power—by faith! It came by a power that does not appear and is not seen and understood by the carnal mind or the scientific intellect. The creation is God's doing. Things came into being by forces which do not appear to man and can in fact be known only by revelation. And as God created all things by faith, even so his created handiwork can be known and understood only by that same power, the power which is faith.[7]

God is intimately involved in and is the moving and directing power behind the Creation. Moreover, many aspects of the Creation can only be understood through revelation—logic, scholarship, and scientific experimentation cannot bring us to a full understanding of it. We need the inspiration and guidance of the Holy Ghost. As Moroni said, by the power of the Holy Ghost we can know the truth of all things (see Moroni 10:5).

Summing up these basic principles:

- The *truths* of revealed religion will agree with the *truths* of science.
- The emphasis must be on *true* religion and *true* science.
- We must recognize our very limited knowledge of the Creation from both a scientific and a scriptural standpoint and humbly recognize that in this mortal sphere we will never come to a complete understanding.
- Revelation has priority over scientific knowledge.
- We should be extremely cautious in attempting to interpret the scriptural accounts of the Creation from a scientific standpoint, since these accounts are not meant to be a scientific treatise on the subject. We need to be very careful not to "wrest the scriptures" through misapplication or faulty interpretation of them.
- We must avoid contention—we can disagree without being disagreeable.
- God is intimately involved in and is the moving and directing power behind the Creation.
- The Creation can only be fully understood through revelation.

QUESTIONS ABOUT THE CREATION

In trying to understand the Creation accounts in the context of science, numerous questions arise. Some of these are:

- How long was each of the creative periods?
- What is the actual age of the earth?
- Was there death among plant and animal life before the Fall of Adam?
- What are all these fossils of strange plants and animals that are no longer found on the earth?

- What about these manlike creatures that lived on the earth thousands or even millions of years ago?
- What about evolution?

Let's examine each of these in turn.

Length of the creative periods. As Elder John A. Widtsoe once pointed out, within the Church there are at least three prevailing positions on the length of the creative periods: (1) each day of the Creation was twenty-four hours, (2) each day of the Creation was actually a thousand years, and (3) the Creation of the earth extended over very long periods, the duration of which we do not yet accurately know.[8] Of these three, the one that seems to agree best with present scientific evidence is "very long periods." A related question is whether each of the creative periods is of the same length. Elder Bruce R. McConkie suggested that "each day [of the Creation] . . . has the duration needed for its purposes. . . . There is no revealed recitation specifying that each of the 'six days' involved in the creation was of the same duration."[9] The scriptural description of separate days or times may well be a way of drawing attention to various aspects of the creative process, which was almost certainly not a series of different, unrelated events but a continuous process in which several different things were happening at the same time.

Those familiar with the temple account of the Creation will recognize that it differs from the scriptural account both in sequence of events as well as what is done on each day. As Elder McConkie stated, "The temple account [of the Creation], for reasons that are apparent to those familiar with its teachings, has a different division of events. It seems clear that the 'six days' are one continuing period and that there is no one place where the dividing lines between the successive events must of necessity be placed."[10]

As I see it, the creative periods extended over vast periods of time—millions or even billions of years in duration. Moreover, these periods were not necessarily separate, successive periods, but a continuous process with many things going on simultaneously.

The age of the earth. This issue is, of course, related to the length of the creative periods. The traditional chronology of the Irish Anglican archbishop James Ussher (1581–1656) places the Fall at 4004 BC. To arrive at this number, Ussher worked back from known dates using the data for births and deaths given for the various patriarchs in the book of Genesis. Unfortunately, these numbers are not consistent in the various manuscripts and versions of the Bible, and we have no way of knowing which, if any, of those are accurate, except as they may occasionally appear in modern scripture (see D&C 107:42–53). A statement of the prophet Nephi, son of Helaman, speaking around 20 BC, suggests that the Fall may have occurred considerably earlier than 4000 BC. Nephi says, "There were many before the days of Abraham who were called by the order of God; yea, even after the order of his Son; and this that it should be shown unto the people, *a great many thousand years before his coming*, that even redemption should come unto them" (Helaman 8:18; emphasis added). Only four thousand years before the coming of Christ does not seem to qualify as "a great many thousand years."

William W. Phelps, who worked as a scribe for Joseph Smith in his translation of the Book of Abraham, made this interesting statement in a letter to William Smith, the prophet's brother: "Eternity, agreeably to the records found in the catacombs of Egypt, has been going on in this system, (not this world) almost two thousand five hundred and fifty five millions of years."[11] An age of 2,555,000,000 years is within an order of magnitude of present scientific estimates of the age of the solar system (around 4.6 billion years).

Scientists have attempted to determine the age the earth and the solar system using a variety of radiometric dating techniques. Radioactive isotopes of elements such as uranium, thorium, potassium, and carbon are unstable. Their radioactivity is the result of their nuclei giving off subatomic particles—protons and neutrons. As a given nucleus emits a particle, it decays, changing into another element or isotope. Ultimately the nucleus reaches a point where it is stable and no longer decays. Uranium, for example, ultimately becomes lead. This radioactive decay occurs at a very predictable rate. The term *half-life* is used to describe this rate. It is the amount of time it takes half of all the atoms of a radioactive substance to decay. This varies considerably from element to element. For uranium-238 the half-life is 4.5 billion years, whereas carbon-14 has a half-life of only 5,730 years. Taking a sample of rock, a scientist can compare the ratio of the radioactive element to its nonradioactive end product in that rock and then calculate its age. The process is, of course, more complex than this—one has to determine how much, if any, of the end-product was present at the beginning, and whether there was some intrusion of material in the intervening time period—but that is the basic idea. Using such techniques, the oldest terrestrial rocks are estimated to be about 3.8 billion years old.[12] Since the earth is very active geologically and is subject to weathering, rocks from its earliest period are not likely to have survived. The oldest rocks found by the Apollo astronauts on the moon, which is not geologically active, and which has no weathering, are around 4.2 billion years old. Radioactive dating of meteorites gives ages of 4.5 to 4.7 billion years old.[13] All of this evidence taken together seems to point to the formation of the solar system and this earth around 4.6 billion years ago.

Death before the Fall. This is an issue that has generated much discussion within the Church, with strong opinions held on both sides. In the late 1920s and early 1930s, Elder Brigham H. Roberts, senior president of the First Council of Seventy, wrote and spoke extensively about his beliefs concerning pre-Adamites and death among plant and animal life before the Fall. His views were strongly opposed by Elder Joseph Fielding Smith of the Quorum of the Twelve. Elder Smith's arguments centered on the passage from 2 Nephi 2:22 that if Adam had not fallen, "all things which were created must have remained in the same state in which they were after they were created;

The Scriptural Accounts of the Creation

and they must have remained forever, and had no end." Each attempted to have his views confirmed by the Church. Both Elder Roberts and Elder Smith formally presented their views to the First Presidency and the Quorum of the Twelve. Then after careful consideration, the First Presidency, in a report dated April 5, 1931, addressed to the Council of the Twelve, the First Council of the Seventy, and the Presiding Bishopric, stated, "Neither side of the controversy has been accepted as doctrine at all."[14] Thus the First Presidency made it clear that the Church has no official stand concerning the existence of pre-Adamites or death among plants and animals before the Fall.

Soon after this, Elder Talmage, who was a geologist called to the Quorum of the Twelve, was invited by the First Presidency to give a talk on the issue. The talk, entitled "The Earth and Man," was given in the Tabernacle on August 9, 1931. In this talk Elder Talmage stated that the earth was extremely ancient. He also confirmed that life and death occurred on the earth long before the coming of man: "But this we know, for both revealed and discovered truth, that is to say, both scripture and science, so affirm—that plant life antedated animal existence, and that animals preceded man on earth. . . . These [plants and animals] lived and died, age after age, while the earth was yet unfit for human habitation."[15]

In November of that same year, 1931, the First Presidency approved the publication of this speech with slight changes, and it appeared in the Church section of the *Deseret News* on November 17.[16] It was subsequently made available as a Church pamphlet and was republished in the *Instructor*.[17]

It is important here to stress that although there may have been death among plants and animals before the Fall, this does not apply to Adam and Eve. The scriptures and the teaching of the Brethren make it absolutely clear that in the Garden of Eden before the Fall, Adam and Eve were not yet subject to death, and it was only by partaking of the forbidden fruit that they became mortal.

Elder Talmage certainly supported the view that among plants and animals there was death before the Fall. If there were no death before the Fall, it would be very difficult to account for all the fossilized remains of now-extinct flora and fauna located in geologic strata all over the earth. In addition, fossils of animals show signs of tumors, rheumatic disorders, arthritis, abscesses, and breakage, and fossils of plants show spot fungi, burls, and insect galls.[18] All these seem to indicate that death and disease were part of living things millions of years ago.

Fossils. Some have tried to account for fossilized remains by suggesting that the earth was formed from parts of other planets and that these fossils are plants and animals from these other worlds. For support, they refer to a quote from Joseph Smith that "this earth was organized or formed out of other planets which were broken up and remodeled and made into the one on which we live."[19] This is not, however, a direct quote from Joseph Smith, but comes from an entry in William Clayton's journal.[20] William McIntire was at the same sermon and recorded what Joseph said somewhat differently: "this Earth has been organized out of portions of other Globes that has ben [sic] Disorganized."[21] Here McIntire uses "globes" rather than "planets," which could refer to any celestial bodies—planets, comets, asteroids, or stars. All the elements out of which this earth is formed, with the exception of hydrogen and some helium, were formed inside stars. The elements from helium to iron were formed in the various stages of fusion a star goes through during its lifetime. Elements heavier than iron are formed primarily in supernova explosions and are then dispersed throughout the galaxy by those explosions. Thus the elements of this earth did indeed come from other "globes" that were disorganized—a supernova is a fairly substantial disorganization! Moreover, it is reasonable to assume that our own earth is typical of what God does in preparing other worlds for his children. Therefore, after an inhabited world has passed through its mortal state, it is not disorganized and thrown into a junk pile for reuse in forming other worlds but is rather resurrected and celestialized.

Another telling argument against fossils being the remains of plants and animals from fragments of other worlds is the sequential way in which they are preserved—in strata or layers. Fossilized plants and animals found at great distances from each other all over the earth are found in equivalent strata, and in the same order within these strata. Were this earth formed from bits and pieces of other planets, this would likely not be the case.

Fossils are simply the remains of life-forms that were once here on the earth and have become extinct. Extinction is a process we are familiar with; we see plants and animals becoming extinct all the time.

Fossils of manlike creatures. What about these manlike creatures that evidently lived on the earth thousands or even millions of years ago? The scriptures do not mention them. What are they? What is our relationship to them? They are certainly creations of our Father in Heaven, but he has not revealed to us their purpose in his plans. In any event, whatever they are, they are not our ancestors, as the First Presidency statement on the origin of man made clear in 1909:

> It is held by some that Adam was not the first man upon the earth, and that the original human being was a development from lower orders of the animal creation. These, however, are the theories of men. The word of the Lord declares that Adam was "the first man of all men" (Moses 1:34), and we are therefore duty bound to regard him as the primal parent of our race. It was shown to the brother of Jared that all men were created in the beginning after the image of God; and whether we take this to mean the spirit or the body, or both, it commits us to the same conclusion: Man began life as a human being, in the likeness of our heavenly Father.[22]

There is no doubt that in the past there were manlike creatures on the earth. But they are not related to us. Hugh Nibley said it well:

> Do not begrudge existence to creatures that looked like men long, long ago, nor deny them a place in God's

affection or even a right to exaltation—for our scriptures allow them such. Nor am I overly concerned as to just when they might have lived, for their world is not our world. They have all gone away long before our people ever appeared. God assigned them their proper times and functions, as he has given me mine—a full-time job that admonishes me to remember his words to the overly eager Moses: "For mine own purpose have I made these things. Here is wisdom and it remaineth in me" (Moses 1:31). It is Adam as my own parent who concerns me.[23]

Organic evolution. The scriptural accounts of the Creation do not give the particulars of the process by which life originated on this earth. But they do make it clear that God was the source and author of all life and was intimately and continuously involved in bringing it forth on this earth. It was not and indeed *cannot* have been, as some scientists maintain, the result of "nothing but a set of individually mindless steps succeeding each other without the help of any intelligent supervision."[24] The details of how God accomplished the placing of life on this earth are not explicitly stated in the scriptures, but his intimate involvement is made absolutely clear. Moreover, he has endowed living organisms with a remarkable degree of adaptability to take advantage of a wide range of environments so they can "fill the earth" as God commanded. Some of the mechanisms described in evolutionary theory may well be the means by which this is accomplished.

In connection with this, we need to recognize what life really is. Life is not simply a self-replicating machine. The scriptures teach us that every living thing consists of both a physical body and a spirit. "And every plant of the field before it was in the earth, and every herb of the field before it grew. For I, the Lord God, created all things, of which I have spoken, spiritually, before they were naturally upon the face of the earth. . . . All things were before created; but spiritually were they created and made according to my word" (Moses 3:5, 7). Indeed it is the process of placing a preexistent spirit into a physical

THE SCRIPTURAL ACCOUNTS OF THE CREATION

body that produces a living soul. "I, the Lord God, formed man from the dust of the ground, and breathed into his nostrils the breath of life; and man became a living soul" (Moses 3:7). This is true not only for man but for animals and plants: "And out of the ground I, the Lord God, formed every beast of the field, and every fowl of the air . . . and they were also living souls; for I, God, breathed into them the breath of life" (Moses 3:19); "And out of the ground made I, the Lord God, to grow every tree, naturally, that is pleasant to the sight of man; and man could behold it. And it became also a living soul" (Moses 3:9).

THE ETERNAL NATURE OF MATTER AND INTELLIGENCE

Latter-day Saints view creation differently than the standard Judeo-Christian doctrine of creation ex nihilo, or out of nothing. The scriptures teach us important and fundamental truths about the universe in which we live. First of all, we learn that "The elements are eternal" (D&C 93:33). God did not create them; they have always existed and will always continue to exist. From a scientific point of view, we might say that matter and energy are eternal, since matter and energy are interchangeable—one can be converted to the other, but neither can be destroyed, as Einstein's famous equation $E = mc^2$ illustrates. Also, "all spirit is matter, but it is more fine or pure" (D&C 131:7). Physical matter and spirit matter are not fundamentally different—spirit matter is simply more refined. Finally, intelligences "have no beginning; they existed before, they shall have no end, they shall exist after, for they are gnolaum, or eternal" (Abraham 3:18), and "intelligence, or the light of truth, was not created or made, neither indeed can be" (D&C 93:29). Intelligence, the ultimate individual identity of every living thing, is also eternal and uncreated.

God's creative work, then, does not produce something out of nothing. It is a process of organizing three eternally existing components—physical matter or energy, spirit matter, and intelligence—utilizing eternal laws that govern this process. "We will go down, for there is space there, and we will take of these materials, and we will make an earth whereon these may dwell" (Abraham 3:24). By so doing, God fulfills his purpose of bringing to pass "the immortality and eternal life of man" (Moses 1:39).

CREATION PLANNED BEFOREHAND

The Abrahamic account reveals another important piece of information about the Creation. It describes a council in heaven where the plans for the Creation were discussed and worked out (see Abraham 5:1–3). President Spencer W. Kimball explained:

> A plan was presented in the great council. Before this earth was created the Lord made a blueprint, as any great contractor will do before constructing. He drew up the plans, wrote the specifications, and presented them. He outlined it and we were associated with him. . . . Our Father called us all together as explained in the scripture, and plans were perfected now for forming an earth. In his own words: "And there stood one among them that was like unto God, and he said unto those who were with him: We will go down, for there is space there, and we will take of these materials, and we will make an earth whereon these may dwell. . . ." (Abraham 3:24) That assemblage included us all. The gods would make land, water, and atmosphere and then the animal kingdom, and give dominion over it all to man. That was the plan. . . . God was the Master-worker, and he created us and brought us into existence.[25]

THE SEVEN CREATIVE PERIODS

The three scriptural accounts all agree that "in the beginning" God created the heavens and the earth. But this is not the beginning of the entire universe, as the account in Moses makes clear: "Behold, I reveal unto you concerning *this* heaven, and *this* earth" (Moses 2:1; emphasis added). This earth is but one of innumerable worlds that our Father in Heaven has created as places of mortal probation for his children, where they learn to develop the divine potential within them to become like him (see Moses 1:35–39; Abraham 3:24–26). Thus the scriptural creation accounts do not describe the creation of the universe, but only the organization of the earth and its surrounding environment—perhaps what we would call the solar system. The universe with its myriad stars, planets, galaxies, and so forth was already there.

Another important point is that Abraham and Moses described the visions they saw of the Creation using language that lacked the specialized scientific vocabulary we now have. Nuclear fusion, gravitation, genetic code, greenhouse effect, atoms, molecules, chemical reactions, and so forth are all part of the creation, but ancient languages lacked terms for these concepts. Much of the challenge of correlating the scriptural accounts of the Creation with scientific knowledge lies in "translating" the language Abraham and Moses used into modern, scientific terminology.

In what follows, I attempt to correlate the events of the Creation as described in scripture with the latest scientific evidence and theories of the formation of the earth and our solar system. The dates I give are not to be considered the last word but rather the best present estimates based on a variety of scientific techniques, especially those derived from the measurement of radioactive decay. At the end of the paper is a chart showing the six creative periods, the events occurring in each, and the estimated dates.

The first period: formation of the solar system (Genesis 1:1–5; Moses 2:1–5; Abraham 4:1–5). We begin with God indicating a region of space where there was sufficient preexisting unorganized matter to organize and form this earth and solar system: "There is space there, and we will take of these materials, and we will make an earth" (Abraham 3:24). The next step in the process was to cause "darkness to come upon the face of the deep" (Moses 2:2), which implies that there was light previous to this—presumably the light of all the myriad stars and galaxies of the universe. Then light was produced: "Let there be light" (Genesis 1:3; Moses 2:3; Abraham 4:3).

And "the earth, after it was formed, was empty and desolate" (Abraham 4:2). We can summarize the events of the first period as follows:

- There was a region of preexistent matter from which God organized this solar system.
- The first step was to cause darkness.
- Then light was produced.
- The earth in its initial state was empty and desolate.

Let us now compare this description with the generally accepted theory of the formation of the solar system. Around 4.7 billion years ago, there was a large cloud of gas and dust with some intrinsic rotation. This cloud, perhaps under the influence of a shock wave from a nearby supernova, began to collapse upon itself due to the mutual gravitational attraction of the constituent gas molecules and dust particles. Since about 75 percent of all the matter in the universe is hydrogen, it was a major component of the cloud. Abraham and Moses perhaps used the term *waters* or *deep* to describe this cloud consisting predominantly of hydrogen. Water, H_2O, is made up of two molecules of hydrogen and one of oxygen. The word *hydrogen* means "water producer" in Greek. As this cloud of gas and dust began to collapse, it became denser and began to block out light; hence the darkness.

As this cloud continued to collapse, the gravitational potential energy of the individual molecules and particles was converted into heat, and eventually in the center of this cloud the density and temperature became high enough to sustain nuclear fusion of hydrogen into helium.[26] There are regions in our galaxy where we see such dark clouds—the Horsehead Nebula in Orion is perhaps the best known—and infrared observations of these clouds show that stars are forming within them.[27]

Regions of higher density within the cloud eventually collapsed to form the planets, asteroids, comets, and other parts of the solar system. Close to the sun, the temperature was higher, which allowed only small, rocky planets like the earth to form. Further out, the temperature was lower, allowing larger, gaseous planets like Jupiter and Saturn to form.[28]

Once fusion started in the core of the protosun, light pressure began to drive out the remaining gas and dust. Stars in this stage of development, i.e. pre-main sequence stars surrounded by dark clouds of gas and dust, have been observed and are called T-Tauri stars.[29] Naked T-Tauri stars are the next stage, in which the cloud has mostly been dispersed.[30] Thus the creation of light seems to refer to the start of nuclear fusion in the core of the sun. It is not, however, until the fourth period that the various "lights" in the heavens become visible, because it took some time for the light pressure of the sun to disperse the dark cloud in which the solar system was formed.

The earth also was formed in this cloud of gas and dust by the accretion of rocky bodies produced within the cloud. This accretion as well as the decay of radioactive elements produced a rapid internal heating, which drove off the initial atmosphere of hydrogen and inert gases and melted the planet. Lighter materials rose to the surface to ultimately form the crust of the earth, and the denser material sank to form the molten nickel-iron core. The earth began to cool, and by about 3.7 billion years ago, the first continents appeared and plate tectonics began.[31]

The events of the first period took place roughly between 4.6 and 3.6 billion years ago, according to the most recent scientific dating techniques.

Second period: formation of the atmosphere (Genesis 1:6-8; Moses 2:6-8; Abraham 4:6-8). In the second period God formed an "expanse" in the midst of the "waters" to separate the waters above from the waters below (Abraham 4:6). This seems to describe the formation of the earth's atmosphere. About 4 billion years ago, volcanic activity caused by interior heating in the earth's crust produced a second atmosphere, containing outgassed water, methane, ammonia, sulfur dioxide, and carbon dioxide.[32] This was also a period of massive bombardment by large meteors and asteroids, which fractured the earth's crust.[33] The scars of this bombardment have mostly been weathered away on the earth, but are still clearly visible on the moon, Mercury, and, to a lesser extent, Mars. After the earth had cooled enough, the earth's ocean basins, which were formed by the combined effect of these bombardments and plate tectonic movement, began to fill with rain that condensed out of the atmosphere.[34]

Beginning about 3.5 billion years ago, photosynthesis by cyanobacteria (primitive one-celled organisms without a distinct nucleus) began to release oxygen into the atmosphere.[35] However, prior to 2 billion years ago, it remained a reducing atmosphere with little free oxygen. Large deposits of reduced minerals such as banded iron chert, detrital pyrite, and uranite could not have formed if even 0.1 percent of the atmosphere had been oxygen. Sometime between 2 and 1.5 billion years ago, levels of oxygen increased to the point that no more reduced minerals formed. From that point on, oxidized minerals are found in the geological record.[36] About 1.5 million years ago, green algae, the first eukaryotes (organisms with nuclei in their cells), began to appear. Green algae are much more efficient photosynthesizers than cyanobacteria, and they began to add more oxygen to the atmosphere until, around 800 million years ago, the oxygen level reached about 5 percent of the present value.[37]

Another important component of the atmosphere was also formed during this period—the ozone layer. Energetic ultraviolet photons began to dissociate water molecules in the atmosphere. The light hydrogen atoms escaped into space while the heavier oxygen atoms remained behind. The oxygen atoms in turn combined to form oxygen molecules (O_2). As O_2 accumulated in the upper atmosphere, it was again dissociated into free oxygen atoms, which in turn combined with other O_2 molecules to form ozone (O_3). The dissociation-association process eventually stabilized, forming the ozone layer. This filtered out harmful ultraviolet light, which not only prevented any further dissociation of water but also allowed life to flourish,[38] since high levels of ultraviolet light are lethal to most living organisms.

The proper mixture of gases in the atmosphere is critically important for sustaining life on the earth. For example, although carbon dioxide and water vapor make up only a very small part of the atmosphere, without them the average temperature of the earth would be about −40° Celsius.[39] It is clear that at various stages of the creative process God carefully arranged for modifications in the earth's atmosphere that would ultimately provide one suited to the animal and plant life now found here.

The earth's magnetic field, produced by its rotating liquid nickel-iron outer core, also helps protect life on the earth's surface. This field deflects the potentially harmful stream of charged particles coming from the sun, called the solar wind, and forms the well-known Van Allen radiation belts.[40]

The events of the second period, in which the present atmosphere of the earth was formed, seemed to have occurred between 4 billion and 600 million years ago, thus overlapping with both the first and the third periods.

Third period: oceans and continents, plant life (Genesis 1:9–13; Moses 2:9–13; Abraham 4:9–13). During the third creative period, the seas were formed and dry land appeared. As indicated above, the water that forms the seas and other bodies of water on the earth came from volcanic outgassing of water vapor, which condensed as rain and began to fill the low-lying areas. Also with the cooling of the crust of the earth around 3.7 billion years ago, the major continental plates formed and the process known as plate tectonics began.[41] As the various continental plates collided with each other, mountain ranges began to form, a process that continues to the present time. The weathering of the earth by rain and wind also caused major changes over time.

Next God prepared the earth for plant life. When it was first formed, the earth was far from being a favorable environment for life. It had an atmosphere of carbon dioxide, hydrogen, sulfur dioxide, methane, and other compounds, but lacked any free oxygen. Plants would thus necessarily be the first living organisms to be placed on the earth because of their ability to convert carbon dioxide into oxygen, which is essential for animal life. The earliest fossil remains in the rocks of the earth, called stromatolites, were formed by cyanobacteria and date back to around 3.5 billion years ago. These remained the dominant form of life until about 1.5 billion years ago,[42] although in Precambrian rocks found in South Africa there are fossil remains of tiny rod-shaped forms that resemble living bacteria in their cell-wall structure.[43] There is some genetic evidence that perhaps archaebacteria preceded the cyanobacteria, but there is no fossil evidence to support this.[44] This means that life appeared on the earth very soon after the crust cooled and solidified.

It is interesting that some scientists have proposed terraforming the planet Venus, converting it to an earthlike environment, by seeding its clouds with cyanobacteria, which would convert the predominantly carbon dioxide atmosphere to oxygen. The reduction of carbon dioxide would in turn reduce the greenhouse effect, and the temperature would drop. Eventually, water vapor in the atmosphere (which contains enough water to cover the entire surface of Venus with 100 inches of water) would condense and fall as rain. Over time the average surface temperature of Venus would drop to around 70 to 80 degrees Fahrenheit, with oceans forming in the depressions.[45] This is, in essence, the process God seems to have used in preparing our earth for more advanced forms of life.

Land plants appeared much later during the Middle Silurian period, some 420 million years ago, and did not become common until near the end of the Devonian, about 360 million years ago.[46] The first appearance of flowering plants (angiosperms) was not until about 120 million years ago.[47] Grasses are not found until around 57 million years ago.[48]

The progressive appearance of plant life[49] on the earth thus stretched over an enormous period of time—from about 3.5 billion years to 57 million years ago, when the variety of plant life was much like what we now have on the earth.

Fourth period: appearance of the sun, moon, and stars (Genesis 1:14–19; Moses 2:14–19; Abraham 4:14–19). During this phase

THE SCRIPTURAL ACCOUNTS OF THE CREATION

of the Creation, God organized the various "lights" in the heavens—the sun, moon, and stars. As explained in the section on the first period, once hydrogen fusion had started in the sun, light pressure would have progressively ejected the remaining gas and dust of the original cloud out of which the solar system formed, thus progressively making these various heavenly bodies visible. This dispersal of the gas and dust occurred within a few million years after fusion started in the protosun.

Organizing the lights for seasons, days, and years seems to refer to the setting of the orbital and rotational periods of the earth and moon. A year is the time it takes for one orbit of the earth around the sun. A month was originally measured as the time period from one new moon to the next, which is based on the orbital period of the moon around the earth. A day is the time it takes the earth to rotate once on its axis. The seasons can also be determined by which constellations are visible at a given period during the year. Moreover, the various seasons are the result of the tilt of the earth's axis with respect to its orbital plane, as well as the eccentricity of its orbit about the sun. All these various aspects of the motions of the earth and the moon had to be fine-tuned to produce the times and seasons we now have.

Fifth period: sea animals and birds (Genesis 1:20–23; Moses 2:20–23; Abraham 4:20–23). God's preparation of the waters to support animal life included providing the proper proportions of dissolved salt and other minerals and ensuring that there would be sources of oxygen and food (plants). In agreement with the scriptural accounts of creation, both plant and animal life appeared first in the oceans. Only in rocks less than 1.5 billion years old are microfossils of eukaryotic cellular organisms found, which are much more complicated than prokaryotic organisms like cyanobacteria.[50] It was only when oxygen levels reached about 5 percent of the present value, some 800 million years ago, that more complex multicellular (metazoan) life began to appear.[51]

About 600 million years ago, at the beginning of the Cambrian period, there was a rapid increase in the variety of higher life forms, called the Cambrian explosion.[52] Around 490 million years ago, exoskeletal animals such as trilobites, brachiopods, and shelled mollusks appeared. By 550 million years ago, the first vertebrates, such as jawless fish and graptolites, appeared.[53]

It was not until 145 million years ago that birds first appeared, and they are, of course, land animals. Why birds are included with sea animals rather than land animals is not clear, but as stated earlier, the separation of the events of the creation into periods is in a sense artificial, since the whole process was a continuous one.

After creating life, God caused the living things "to be fruitful and multiply, and fill the waters . . . and . . . to multiply in the earth" (Abraham 4:22). This refers to the prolific capability God designed into all life to adapt itself to an incredible variety of environmental conditions and fill every ecological niche.

Sixth period: land animals and man (Genesis 1:24–31; Moses 2:24–31; Abraham 4:24–31). In the sixth and final period of creation, God prepared the land to be an environment conducive to life. This included the weathering of rocks to produce soil, the establishment of land plants to provide food and oxygen for land animals, and so on. As this process progressed, more complex forms of animal life could be supported. The fossil records show that about 370 million years ago, amphibians first appeared. By 340 million years ago the earliest reptiles (cotylosaurs) were present, and by 320 million years ago mammal-like reptiles (pelycosaurs) were found. Winged insects appeared around 310 million years ago, and dinosaurs came on the scene about 240 million years ago. By 220 million years ago, there was a large variety of mammal-like reptiles, but it was not until about 90 million years ago that marsupials (animals with pouches like a kangaroo) and placentals (animals in which the young develop in a womb with a placenta) appeared.[54]

Around 65 million years ago, at the end of the Cretaceous period, there was a period of mass extinctions, in which dinosaurs and many other kinds of life disappeared. This may have been caused by a giant asteroid impact.[55] The fossil record also shows other major extinction events such as the Permian around 250 million years ago.[56]

The first primates appeared 62 million years ago, and by 60 million years ago there was a great diversity of mammal types. Rodents first arrived on the scene about 45 million years ago, and hominids (manlike creatures) about 19 million years ago.[57]

The first appearance of *Homo sapiens sapiens* (human beings) and *Homo sapiens neanderthalensis* (Neanderthals) seems to have been about 125,000 years ago, when fossils of both are found. This was at about the temperature maximum of the last interglacial period. Around 30,000 years ago, Neanderthals seem to have become extinct. By 18,000 years ago, the last ice age reached its maximum, with glaciers covering large areas of northern Europe and North America.[58] About 11,600 years ago, there was a rapid warming, and the ice sheets melted, producing catastrophic flooding of the Mississippi Valley and other places.[59] Could this have been the biblical flood?

This final stage of the creation seems to have covered a period from about 370 million years ago to the point when Adam and Eve were first placed on the earth.

Seventh period: Sabbath (Genesis 2:1–3; Moses 3:1–3; Abraham 5:1–3). The seventh period is actually not part of the creation, but is the rest period after the work was done. We have no information as to how long it lasted.

CONCLUSION

This paper is certainly not meant to be the final word on the incredibly complex subject of the Creation from both a scriptural and scientific perspective. Advances in science and new revelation could alter some, or even many, of the conclusions made here. What is clear, however, is that there are no insurmountable areas of disagreement between the scriptural accounts of the Creation and our present scientific understanding. When looked at from the proper perspective, there is, in fact, a remarkable degree of agreement. Indeed, *true* religion and *true* science will always be in harmony.

Possible Chronology of the Events of Creation

Period	Activity	Details	Years before present
First	Formation of solar system	Earliest meteoroids formed	4.7 billion
		Solar system formed	4.6 billion
		Oldest lunar rocks	4.2 billion
		Oldest terrestrial rocks	3.8 billion
Second	Formation of atmosphere	First (original) atmosphere	4.0 billion
		Volcanic activity formed second atmosphere	4.0 billion
		Blue-green algae begin to produce O_2 in atmosphere	3.5 billion
		Oxygen level reaches 5 percent of present value	800 million
Third	Formation of continents and ocean Plant life	Plate tectonics begins	3.7 billion
		Cyanobacteria (blue-green algae)	3.5 billion
		Green algae	1.5 billion
		Land plants	420 million
		Flowering plants	120 million
		Grasses	57 million
Fourth	Appearance of sun, moon, and stars	Light pressure from the sun clears out residual gas and dust	4.5 to 4.4 billion
Fifth	Sea animals and birds	Cambrian explosion of complex life forms	600 million
		Exoskeleton animals	590 million
		Vertebrates	550 million
		Birds	150 million
Sixth	Land animals	Amphibians	370 million
		Reptiles	340 million
		Mammal-like reptiles	320 million
		Marsupials and placentals	90 million
		Primates	62 million
		Rodents	45 million
		Hominids	19 million

NOTES

This chapter is modified from Michael D. Rhodes and J. Ward Moody, "Astronomy and the Creation in the Book of Abraham," in *Astronomy, Papyrus, and Covenant*, ed. John Gee and Brian M. Hauglid (Provo, UT: Institute for the Study and Preservation of Ancient Religious Texts, 2005), 17–36.

1. Brigham Young, in *Journal of Discourses* (London: Latter-day Saints' Book Depot, 1854–86), 17:53.
2. *The Teachings of Harold B. Lee*, ed. Clyde J. Williams (Salt Lake City: Bookcraft, 1996), 341.
3. Bruce R. McConkie, "Christ and the Creation," *Ensign*, June 1982, 10.
4. James E. Talmage, "The Earth and Man," *Instructor*, December 1965, 475.
5. Boyd K. Packer, "The Law and the Light," in *The Book of Mormon: Jacob through Words of Mormon, to Learn with Joy*, ed. Monte S. Nyman and Charles D. Tate Jr. (Provo, UT: Religious Studies Center, Brigham Young University, 1990), 8.
6. *Teachings of Gordon B. Hinckley* (Salt Lake City, Utah: Deseret Book, 1997), 549.
7. Bruce R. McConkie, *Doctrinal New Testament Commentary* (Salt Lake City: Bookcraft, 1970), 3:196.
8. John A. Widtsoe, *Evidences and Reconciliations* (Salt Lake City: Bookcraft, 1960), 146.
9. Bruce R. McConkie, "Christ and the Creation," *Ensign*, June 1982, 11.
10. McConkie, "Christ and the Creation," 11.
11. William W. Phelps, "The Answer," *Times and Seasons*, January 1844, 758. This number may have been arrived at as follows: 7,000 years of the Lord's time of 1,000 years per day (i.e., 2,555,000,000 = 1,000 × 365 × 7,000).
12. Cesare Emiliani, *The Scientific Companion* (New York: John Wiley & Sons, 1988), 197.
13. Frank H. Shu, *The Physical Universe: An Introduction to Astronomy* (Mill Valley, CA: University Science Books, 1982), 462.
14. James B. Allen, "The Story of *The Truth, the Way, the Life*," in B. H. Roberts, *The Truth, the Way, the Life: An Elementary Treatise on Theology*, ed. John W. Welch, 2nd ed. (Provo, UT: BYU Studies, 1996), 709. This article has an extensive description of this controversy between Elders Roberts and Smith, as well as supporting documentation.
15. James E. Talmage, "The Earth and Man," *Instructor*, December, 1965, 474–75.
16. Allen, "The Story of *The Truth, the Way, the Life*," 711.
17. James E. Talmage, "The Earth and Man," *Instructor*, December, 1965, 474–77; January, 1966, 9–11, 15.

18. Patricia V. Rich and others, *The Fossil Book: A Record of Prehistoric Life*, 2nd ed. rev. (Mineola, NY: Dover, 1996), 15.
19. Franklin D. Richards and James A. Little, *A Compendium of the Doctrines of the Gospel* (Salt Lake City: Deseret News, 1882), 287.
20. *The Words of Joseph Smith: The Contemporary Accounts of the Nauvoo Discourses of the Prophet Joseph*, ed. Andrew F. Ehat and Lyndon W. Cook (Orem, UT: Grandin Book, 1991), 60.
21. *Words of Joseph Smith*, 61; original spelling, punctuation, and grammar retained.
22. Joseph F. Smith, John R. Winder, and Anthon H. Lund, "The Origin of Man," in *Messages of the First Presidency*, ed. James R. Clark (Salt Lake City: Bookcraft, 1965), 4:205.
23. Hugh W. Nibley, "Before Adam," in *Old Testament and Related Studies* (Salt Lake City: Deseret Book, 1986), 82.
24. Daniel C. Dennet, *Darwin's Dangerous Idea: Evolution and the Meanings of Life* (New York: Simon and Schuster, 1995), 59.
25. *Teachings of Spencer W. Kimball* (Salt Lake City: Deseret Book, 1982), 29.
26. For details on this process, see Michael Zeilik, Stephen A. Gregory, and Elske V. Smith, "The Interstellar Medium and Star Birth," in *Introductory Astronomy and Astrophysics*, 3rd ed. (New York: Saunders College, 1992), 366–390; see also Bradley W. Carroll and Dale A. Ostlie, "The Process of Star Formation," in *An Introduction to Modern Astrophysics* (New York: Addison-Wesley, 1996), 437–76.
27. Zeilik, Gregory, and Smith, "Interstellar Medium," 390.
28. Zeilik, Gregory, and Smith, "Interstellar Medium," 141–45.
29. Zeilik, Gregory, and Smith, "Interstellar Medium," 341–42; Carroll and Ostlie, *Introduction to Modern Astrophysics*, 468–75.
30. Zeilik, Gregory, and Smith, "Interstellar Medium," 391.
31. Zeilik, Gregory, and Smith, "Interstellar Medium," 76.
32. Zeilik, Gregory, and Smith, "Interstellar Medium," 76.
33. Zeilik, Gregory, and Smith, "Interstellar Medium," 76.
34. Zeilik, Gregory, and Smith, "Interstellar Medium," 76.
35. Shu, *Physical Universe*, 494.
36. Rich and others, *Fossil Book*, 79.
37. Emiliani, *Scientific Companion*, 156.
38. Shu, *Physical Universe*, 492.
39. Emiliani, *Scientific Companion*, 157.

40. Zeilik, Gregory, and Smith, "Interstellar Medium," 72–74.
41. Zeilik, Gregory, and Smith, "Interstellar Medium," 76.
42. Emiliani, *Scientific Companion*, 151.
43. Rich and others, *Fossil Book*, 91.
44. Emiliani, *Scientific Companion*, 151.
45. Adrian Berry, *The Next Ten Thousand Years: A Vision of Man's Future in the Universe* (New York: New American Library, 1974), 90–93; Carl Sagan first suggested the idea in "The Planet Venus," *Science* 133, no. 3456 (March 24, 1961): 849–58.
46. Rich and others, *Fossil Book*, 67.
47. Rich and others, *Fossil Book*, 33–35.
48. Rich and others, *Fossil Book*, 33–35.
49. I recognize that classifying cyanobacteria and green algae as plants is not in accordance with modern biological classification schemes, which now recognize five kingdoms. But, as was stated above, the scriptures are not meant as textbooks of geology, biology, etc. The cyanobacteria and algae perform the same function as more complex plant life in that they convert carbon dioxide to free oxygen.
50. Shu, *Physical Universe*, 495.
51. Emiliani, *Scientific Companion*, 159.
52. Shu, *Physical Universe*, 497.
53. Rich and others, *Fossil Book*, 33–35.
54. Rich and others, *Fossil Book*, 33–35.
55. Rich and others, *Fossil Book*, 33–35.
56. Rich and others, *Fossil Book*, 247, 483.
57. Rich and others, *Fossil Book*, 33–35.
58. Emiliani, *Scientific Companion*, 195.
59. Emiliani, *Scientific Companion*, 195; Rich and others, *Fossil Book*, 617.

Detail of *Charles Robert Darwin*, by John Collier and detail of *The Prophet and the Patriarch*, by Sutcliffe Maudsley, 1847.

Michael F. Whiting

Evolution and the Gospel: Seeking Grandeur in This View of Life

There is grandeur in this view of life, with its several powers, having been originally breathed by the Creator into a few forms or into one; and that, whilst this planet has gone cycling on according to the fixed law of gravity, from so simple a beginning endless forms most beautiful and most wonderful have been, and are being, evolved.[1]

Insects fascinate me. One of my earliest memories comes from when I was five and stopped along the edge of a vacant lot to catch butterflies that were feeding on a patch of dandelions. I still remember the excitement of catching a monarch butterfly with my cupped hands, carefully pinching the tips of its wings between my fingers, and watching it unwind its long proboscis. I collected insects in my teenage years, and there was hardly a time while I was growing up that I did not have some beetle or moth in the freezer, waiting to be mounted as the newest addition to my insect collection. My parents were patient with my entomological predilections because they assumed it was just a phase I would pass through on my way to finding something respectable to do with my life. I have yet to do so.

Michael F. Whiting is director of the DNA Sequencing Center and an associate professor of integrative biology at Brigham Young University.

But how could one not love insects? Nature is complex, beautiful, and full of a wide diversity of forms, and in no place is this more apparent than when one takes a moment to contemplate the insect. I cannot look at insects without being amazed at their sheer beauty, their stunning colors, and their bizarre forms. I have spent a good portion of my life in pursuit of insects, from the metallic-green praying mantids of the Malaysian rainforest to the walking sticks of Papua New Guinea to the ice bugs that are only rarely encountered at night, crawling across the glaciers of the Pacific Northwest. There are roughly 1.7 million described species on the planet, and over one million of these are insects. Entomologists estimate that there are anywhere from two to twenty million more insect species yet to be discovered, so there is plenty of work to be done. In the 1920s, there were about four hundred thousand species of beetles described, and this number was vastly larger than any other group of organisms. It is said that the naturalist J. B. S. Haldane was once asked by a theologian what he might infer about the nature of the Creator based on his wide-ranging study of life. Haldane reportedly replied, tongue in cheek, that the Creator had "an inordinate fondness for beetles."[2]

But certainly beauty in nature is not limited to just the insects. We draw inspiration from communing with nature, and there is something that brings us closer to the divine as we contemplate the beauty and the glory of creation. My lifelong study of insects has never diminished the sense of awe I feel for the natural world and has only enhanced my admiration and reverence for a supreme Creator who made such biological diversity in a supremely intelligent way. I believe in a Creator who put in place a series of laws that led to the magnificent diversity of forms, behaviors, and intricate interconnections that we see on the earth today. I stand in awe of these products of the Creation, and my studies lead me to reverence the creative process itself: the very thing I am trying to decipher through my own studies. As Darwin expressed at the close of *On the Origin of Species*, I feel there is "grandeur in this view of life."

However, I am keenly aware that this is not the way that many people view evolutionary biology. Some members of the Latter-day Saint faith believe that evolution stands in direct opposition to basic gospel principles, while others consider it a threat to our youth. But I find that most members are just curious as to how someone can be an evolutionary biologist, a member of the Church, and a BYU professor. The purpose of this short essay is to provide a brief outline of why I find my studies in evolutionary biology to be faith affirming. I will not attempt to provide an extensive history of evolution and the Church, nor will I delve into mysteries and attempt to reconcile every aspect of my science with my religion. Both are interesting topics but beyond the scope of this work. My goal is to describe as clearly as I can why my studies in evolution are exciting from a scientific standpoint and also enhance my understanding of the Creation.

PATTERN AND PROCESS

Many critics of evolution portray evolutionary theory as a series of made-up stories that require just as much faith to believe in as any religion requires. They point out that evolution is only a theory, which they equate with a guess or speculation, not recognizing that all science is built on theory and that the so-called laws of science are not qualitatively different from theories—they are simply theories that have stood up to many challenges and (as of yet) have not been refuted. A good theory must be descriptive, predictive, and refutable; that is, it must describe current observations and predict observations that have yet to be made, and it must be possible to collect a set of observations that would disprove it. Evolution passes the muster on all accounts. In fact, evolutionary theory is widely considered to be one of the most successful scientific theories ever proposed because of its ability to explain the biological observations of Darwin's day and its continued ability to elegantly explain a plethora of biological observations that Darwin could not even fathom, including the genomic-based research of today.

Scientists embrace evolution because it is the central underlying concept in all of biology, and it provides us with an extensive set of tools to address real-world problems such as devising strategies to rescue threatened species and protecting humans against infectious agents. There are few scientific theories that have so successfully summarized such an abundance of observations with such an economy of descriptive processes. This is why evolutionary theory is unabashedly not just good science but great science.

There is also confusion expressed by some about how a historical science such as evolutionary biology can learn anything about the past. The first thing to recognize is that biological diversity is not a random assemblage of forms; there is order and pattern in nature. Much of science lies in documenting the patterns we observe in nature and then postulating processes that may account for those patterns. There is in fact a direct connection between pattern and process: a process is simply a set of mechanisms that give rise to a pattern. In many cases, we can infer the process by a careful observation of the pattern. So just because we might not be physically present to observe a process does not mean we cannot learn something about it, because we can effectively learn about a process by studying the patterns that it creates.

Let me illustrate the connection between process and pattern with a simple example. When my daughter was two years old, she was a messy eater. One day I gave her some chocolate pudding and teddy bear crackers to eat as she sat in her high chair and then stepped out of the room for a moment. When I walked back in, I discovered a striking new pattern: chocolate smears with vestiges of mangled teddy bears artistically sprinkled across her high chair tray. This was a pattern, and a much more interesting pattern than the one that existed before I left the room. As a parent, my immediate thought was to clean it all up. But as a scientist, I was left to wonder, "What processes gave rise to this pattern?" Notice I did not ask *who* gave rise to the pattern; I was pretty confident I knew who the culprit was. I was only interested in discovering the specific processes associated with forming the pattern. For instance, I might hypothesize that the ridges formed in the pudding in the middle of the tray were created by finger smearing as opposed to elbow smearing or face smearing. And the fact that the teddy bears did not have any pudding on their dorsal surfaces suggests that they were applied to the pattern only after the pudding smearing had taken place. Now remember, I was not there; I did not see the process in action. But I was able to infer something about a process I did not observe by carefully examining the pattern that the process created. Patterns provide evidence for deciphering processes.

The notion that patterns exist in nature—and that they can be organized in a regular and orderly fashion—is not a new idea. Aristotle was a keen observer of nature, and he thought deeply and profoundly about how his observations should be logically organized. He thought that all of nature could be organized into a ladder, the "Systema Naturae." At the base of this ladder are the simple plants that were not much different from nonliving matter. At the pinnacle was the human species, and each group of organisms had a place within the hierarchy that roughly corresponded to their level of complexity. But it was a ladder and not an escalator. There was no notion that any species could transform into any other, nor was there any idea of progression. There was a place for every species, and every species had its place.

Let us now jump to the seventeenth century and consider for a moment a body of thought that became prevalent with the writings of John Ray. Ray was a Cambridge professor who championed the idea of natural theology. Natural theology taught that by studying a creation, one could learn about the attributes and characteristics of the Creator. Living things adapt to their environments, which for Ray was a sign of God's design and benevolence. So why does a lion have sharp claws? It is because God could not let lions go hungry. Why do the birds sing in the trees? It is because they are singing the praises of a just Creator. Ray affirmed powerfully that nature was a worthy subject for study and reason and that such activity was pleasing to God. Ray, of course, was not the first natural theologian, and we have from Alma a similar sentiment: "Yea, and all things denote that there is a God; yea, even the earth, and all things that are upon the face of it, yea, and its motion, yea, and also all the planets which move in their regular form do witness that there is a Supreme Creator" (Alma 30:44).

CHARLES DARWIN

Darwin was born February 12, 1809, in Shrewsbury, England. This was the same day that Abraham Lincoln was born and was only three years after the birth of Joseph Smith. These three men—Smith, Lincoln, and Darwin—were all contemporaries who profoundly changed mankind's view of religion, politics, and science. Darwin was in fact influenced by many of the same religious and social dynamics that surrounded Joseph Smith. It is interesting that these men were contemporaries during a time when the Lord saw fit to rain down knowledge upon the earth.

Charles Darwin provided profound insights into the nature of nature. He saw what everyone else saw, but he provided a new way of putting the information together. He was a meticulous observer, and he managed to digest and synthesize a tremendous amount of information. The theories he produced continue to influence everything we do in biology today.

I might mention here that some portray Darwin as a man eager to destroy faith and tear down religion. These people are like the detractors who paint Joseph Smith and the history of the Church with similar brushstrokes. Within the Church, I have occasionally heard members equate Darwin with Korihor, the anti-Christ from the Book of Mormon. But these caricatures are too simplistic and not true to the record. (It seems to me that members of the Church should be particularly sensitive to the misrepresentation of mid-nineteenth-century historical figures in order to push a particular agenda forward.) Certainly the ideas that sprang from Darwin's work had a profound influence on religious thought and still continue to do so, but by all accounts Darwin was a loving father and a kind man, afraid of confrontation, and someone who would much rather study the mining habits of earthworms than be involved in a debate over science and religion. Darwin was a complex man, and many lengthy biographies have delved into factors in his life that may have influenced his scientific ideas, including his faith, but at his very core, Darwin was simply a scientist trying to explain patterns in the natural world, and the notion that he had a hidden agenda to destroy religion is simply wrong.

In 1859 Darwin published *On the Origin of Species*, which is packed with Darwin's observations and the connections he tried to make between those observations. For the first time, someone was able to successfully draw a connection between the jaws of a stag beetle, the ornate feathers of the peacock, the blooming patterns of plums, and the behavior of honeybees, and to tie all of these observations to literally thousands more. Moreover, Darwin recognized the hierarchy of similarity among all species. A housefly looks like a fruit fly (they both have one set of wings for flight), and both flies share similarities with a beetle (they all have six legs), but these insects do not look much like a rhinoceros, and as a group, they look even less like dandelions. Darwin recognized that all species can in fact be tied together into a pattern that unfolds into a great tree of life, and he explained these and other patterns with a coherent set of processes—natural selection, descent with modification, and sexual selection—all of which form the basis for modern evolutionary research.

WHERE DID ALL THE GRANDEUR GO?

From the moment that Darwin formally published his ideas of descent with modification in his book *On the Origin of Species*, there has been a nearly steady stream of public outcry over evolution; here we are more than 150 years later, and the outcry has largely not abated. What happened to the grandeur in Darwin's view of life? What is it about evolution that causes blood pressure to rise? How many times have you heard someone express a passionate opinion on one side or the other of the subject of evolution? I have never witnessed people on a bus arguing about the laws of thermodynamics, but I have overheard heated arguments about evolution. I have yet to meet a student who is repulsed by the periodic table of elements or links it to the rampant degradation of society, but I continually encounter both reactions to evolution. Legislators do not push the teaching of an "intelligent falling theory" as a scientific alternative to gravity, but we encounter efforts to teach "intelligent design" as a scientific alternative to evolution. People who are normally oblivious to the theories used to describe observations in chemistry, physics, geology, or any other scientific field somehow have developed strong opinions about the theories evolutionary biologists use to describe observations in the natural world. Evolution is in fact the only scientific theory of which I am aware that has ever been battled over in the Supreme Court, and many organizations engage all their efforts and influence to renounce it.

THE CHURCH AND EVOLUTION

Of course, The Church of Jesus Christ of Latter-day Saints has not been immune to this controversy, and one need not dive deep into Church history to recognize that different Church leaders at different times have expressed very different views on evolution. I am not aware of any other scientific idea that has generated as many diverse views in the Church as evolution has, and very often the discussion of this wide range of ideas has resulted in more heat than light. When I teach evolution in the BYU classroom, I must often curtail students who begin selectively quoting their favorite General Authorities and pitting the quotations of one against another, as if one General Authority could beat the other up. While I am grateful that the Church has never expressed the same extreme views about evolution as have other religious denominations, there still persists a belief that evolutionary ideas and Church doctrine are fundamentally hostile to each other and that the full acceptance of one requires the compromise of the other. I often encounter individuals who question whether one can be a faithful member of the Church and also study evolutionary biology. Others have expressed to me that it is impossible to reconcile scientific theories concerning the creation of the world with fundamental gospel principles, and that any attempt to do so is flawed from the beginning. I have also met with individuals for whom evolution is really not an issue, and while they are curious about my perspective, they simply have decided that there are more important things to worry about.

It is not surprising that given the wide range of opinions on evolution as expressed by Church leaders at various times, many members desire a pronouncement of the Church's official position on evolution. When I was an undergraduate student at BYU in the 1980s, I vividly recall receiving one set of General Authority statements on evolution that were assembled by biology professors and another very different set from professors in Religious Education. These compilations generally did not reflect the full spectrum of statements that had been given on the matter but instead supported only the particular positions held by the professors who assembled them. In 1992, under the direction of the university's board of trustees, which consisted of the First Presidency, many members of the Quorum of the Twelve, and other General Authorities, a packet on evolution was assembled and made available to BYU faculty and students. This packet consisted of all statements issued by the First Presidency on the subject of evolution and the origin of man. It included an introductory cover page approved by the board of trustees and four official statements: the First Presidency statement titled "The Origin of Man," which was released in 1909; a First Presidency message from 1910 that included brief comments relative to these topics; the statement titled "Mormon View of Evolution" published in 1925; and the article on evolution published in the *Encyclopedia of Mormonism* in 1992.[3] A thorough analysis of these statements is beyond the scope of this short essay, but I will briefly highlight some points that resonate the most with me.

The introductory cover page makes two important points that help to put the other statements in their proper context: "Although there has never been a formal declaration from the First Presidency addressing the general matter of organic evolution as a process for development of biological species, these documents make clear the official position of the Church regarding the origin of man" (paragraph 1). "Various views have been expressed by other Church leaders on this subject over many decades; however, formal statements by the First Presidency are the definitive source of official Church positions" (paragraph 3). It is thus clear that these official statements are not centered on whether evolutionary theory does an adequate job of describing a wide range of biological observations, but rather focus on the origin of man. Moreover, it makes it abundantly clear that any statement outside of the four included in the packet are views of their respective authors, no matter how passionate or authoritative they may appear, and do not constitute any official Church position.

The 1909 statement was prepared in anticipation of the centennial celebration of Charles Darwin's birth and the fiftieth anniversary of the publication of *On the Origin of Species*, and it is by far the longest one in the packet (2,737 words). It quotes extensively from Moses, Ether, and other scriptures and "proclaims man to be the direct and lineal offspring of Deity" (paragraph 34). There is a bit of anti-evolution tone in statements such as this: "It is held by some that Adam was not the first man upon this earth, and that the original human being was a development from lower orders of the animal creation. These, however, are the theories of men" (paragraph 31).

The 1910 statement comes from a First Presidency Christmas Message. It is much shorter (99 words), and can be quoted here in its entirety:

> Diversity of opinion does not necessitate intolerance of spirit, nor should it embitter or set rational being against

each other. The Christ taught kindness, patience, and charity.

Our religion is not hostile to real science. That which is demonstrated, we accept with joy; but vain philosophy, human theory and mere speculations of men, we do not accept nor do we adopt anything contrary to divine revelation or to good common sense. But everything that tends to right conduct, that harmonizes with sound morality and increases faith in Deity, finds favor with us no matter where it may be found.

The 1925 statement was released during the fury of media attention surrounding the Scopes "monkey trial" and is specifically titled "Mormon View of Evolution." This statement quotes exclusively from the 1909 statement, but it is about one-fifth the length and omits all of the anti-evolution sentiments in the 1909 statement, including paragraph 31 (quoted above).

The 1992 *Encyclopedia of Mormonism* statement is short (250 words) and emphasizes that "the scriptures tell why man was created, but they do not tell how, though the Lord has promised that he will tell that when he comes again (D&C 101:32–33)" (paragraph 3). It further states: "Upon the fundamental doctrines of the Church we are all agreed. Our mission is to bear the message of the restored gospel to the world. Leave geology, biology, archaeology, and anthropology, no one of which has to do with the salvation of the souls of mankind, to scientific research, while we magnify our calling in the realm of the Church" (paragraph 3).

So what can one take from all of these statements? The 1910 statement makes clear that there are two major conditions for accepting a scientific theory or idea "with joy": (1) the ideas espoused must be good science and not just mere speculation and (2) the ideas should not contradict revelation or "common sense" but increase faith in God and harmonize with sound morality. Regarding the first condition, evolutionary biology is solid science by any measure. Regarding the second condition, I would suggest that whether evolution contradicts revelation or promotes faith is largely a matter of perspective. Some have passionately expressed the feeling that any sort of biological connection between humans and other species on the planet is degrading and leads to immorality and the corruption of society. Others have suggested that since evolutionary biology does not specifically recognize God as Creator to explain biological observations, it is therefore hostile to the notion of a divine creation. I believe both points of view are extreme. God is not invoked to explain biological phenomena in evolutionary biology for precisely the same reason he is absent from other scientific theories: God is not a testable scientific hypothesis that is open to refutation with empirical evidence.

From my perspective, I find it ennobling to think that I share some sort of biological heritage with all of God's glorious creations, and I am amazed to contemplate a Creator who made sets of laws that guided the creation of the world and led to the outpouring of biological diversity. All of my studies lead me to believe in a God who created a creation with the ability to create and modify itself. There clearly is sufficient latitude in these statements to allow the exploration of evolutionary biology without surrendering faith.

ARE MORMONS CREATIONISTS?

There has been a temptation for some members of the Church to place us in the same category as religions that identify themselves as creationists. I tell my students that Mormons are creationists in the same way we are born-again Christians. Does the Church have a doctrine of being "born again"? It certainly does, but it is so radically different from churches that label themselves as born-again Christians that we have not adopted the name because we do not embrace the dogmas associated with being "born again." Likewise, the Latter-day Saint doctrine of creation is sufficiently distinct from those religious groups that label themselves "creationists" that I am grateful the Church has not adopted this label.

One of the most vocal advocates for creationism is Henry Morris, who is associated with the Creation Research Institute. He states, "Since nothing in the world has been created since the end of the creation period, everything must then have been created by means or methods of processes which are no longer in operation and which we therefore cannot study by any of the means or methods of science. We are limited exclusively to divine revelation as to the date of creation, the duration of creation, the method of creation, and every other question concerning the creation."[4] In stark contrast to 1910 First Presidency statement, Morris's view is hostile to real science and specifically requires the belief in doctrines that Latter-day Saints would be uncomfortable with. These doctrines include a belief in ex nihilo ("out of nothing") creation, which was specifically rejected by Joseph Smith, biblical literalism that requires a literal interpretation of such things as time periods, biblical exclusivity that excludes other revelatory sources or scientific investigation as providing insight into creation, and the sole authority of the Bible as the comprehensive source of all details on creation.

Recently there has been a movement in the United States seeking to teach "intelligent design" as a scientific alternative to evolution. Intelligent design is based on the (flawed) notion that there are certain features in the biological world that are too complex to be explained via evolution and that the probability of evolution giving rise to complexity is so vanishingly small that it is simply not possible. Consequently, they argue, the only scientific explanation for biological complexity is that there must be an intelligent designer working behind the scenes. The attempt to mandate the teaching of intelligent design in public schools led to a lengthy trial centered in Dover, Pennsylvania, in 2004. The overwhelming evidence during the trial established that intelligent design was a mere relabeling of the type of creationism described above and that it is not a scientific alternative to evolution. So while the Latter-day Saints do indeed have a doctrine of creation and certainly a belief in a Supremely Intelligent Creator, we are neither creationists nor proponents of intelligent design because both labels come with unwanted and uncomfortable doctrinal baggage.

MY OPINION ON EVOLUTION

Being a Latter-day Saint evolutionary biologist always leads to interesting conversations. Whenever I visit a new ward in my travels, a typical conversation goes something like this:

I am asked, "What do you do for work?"

I respond, "I study insects."

I see an eyebrow raise, and then I am asked, "What is it about insects that you study?"

I respond, "Their genealogy or evolutionary relationships."

"Well, who pays you to do that?"

I respond, "BYU."

Their eyes open wide, their jaws drop, and I can tell what they are thinking. Their first thought is, "Does the Church have some new family history program that I haven't heard of?" But invariably their second thought is, "How can you do that at BYU? Isn't evolution diametrically opposed to the teachings of the Church?"

For me, evolution is simply the scientific study of the underlying mechanics of the creative process. It studies the patterns of creation and seeks to define the processes which gave rise to these patterns. It does not preclude the existence of God, nor does it challenge his role in the Creation. Recall the analogy of my daughter that I used earlier. I knew who was responsible for smearing her food; I was only interested in how she did it. But by studying the pattern she created, I learned something about her. She is messy. Perhaps she is creative. Or maybe she just really likes pudding. This is very much the way I view my own research. I know who is responsible for the Creation, but my research focuses on learning something about how it was done. Much like a natural theologian, I seek to learn something about the Creator by studying the Creation; but I move it back one step by asking, what does the creative process teach me about the nature of the Creator?

We often glory in the end products of the creative process: all the species that surround us and stun us with their vibrant colors, amazing behavior, and peculiar features. And we are right to do so; there is something that brings us closer to the divine by contemplating the grand diversity of life. But I think we do not give the Creator enough credit for his wisdom and divine forethought in establishing the laws that have led to this diversity. I believe the Lord set certain laws in place which resulted in a world filled with diversity, beauty, and form, with each species interacting with every other, tied together in a glorious whole. Now I do not understand what all these laws are—this is why I study the things I do—but from what little I know, I am struck with amazement at just how clever this creation is.

All of my studies lead me to believe that the Lord created the earth in a supremely intelligent fashion. Consider for a moment DNA. There are four basic blocks that comprise the DNA molecule. From a biological standpoint, the only difference between every species that inhabits the planet is the pattern in which these four blocks are arranged in long strings, like numbers in a telephone book. When we look at how these blocks are arranged via modern DNA research, we get a very consistent story of the past. Alma was right: "By small and simple things are great things brought to pass" (Alma 37:6).

Let me put it another way. I can observe a collection of clay pots arranged in a row and marvel at the diversity of shapes, forms, and colors. I can admire the potter, and even try to learn something about how those pots were made. But I fail miserably when I try to make a pot, and I marvel at the skill displayed when I watch a really excellent potter throw a really excellent pot. It is not as easy as it looks, and not just anyone can do it. So I admire the potter, the pot, and the skill required—the process—to make a pot. It seems to me that it is the knowledge, the process, the skill possessed by the potter that is truly what is most impressive here. And who am I to tell the potter how a pot can and cannot be made, seeing that I cannot make one myself? I can likewise marvel at the skill of a Creator who has made a very excellent creation in a very excellent way. I likewise am not comfortable in setting a limit on the divinely clever processes the Creator used to bring about the Creation, seeing that none of these processes have been described in revelation.

Recall that Joseph Smith and Darwin were contemporaries. While Darwin was in the midst of his travels on the HMS *Beagle*, Joseph Smith received the following revelation: "Yea, verily I say unto you, in that day when the Lord shall come, he shall reveal all things—things which have passed, and hidden things which no man knew, things of the earth, by which it was made, and the purpose and the end thereof—things most precious, things that are above, and things that are beneath, things that are in the earth, and upon the earth, and in heaven" (D&C 101:32–34). The Lord indicates that the day will come when he will reveal more about the earth and how it was made, along with many other precious things. However, I do not think that this verse means that we can learn nothing about creation until the Lord comes or that we should not try. To claim that we should not attempt to learn anything about the creative process in this life through study and effort is the same to me as the claim that we should not strive to learn anything about the nature of God until he comes and reveals himself to us.

THE HARD QUESTIONS

I have not attempted in this short essay to address all of the mysteries that arise when one tries to reconcile current understanding of the scriptures with current understanding of evolutionary biology. I have not delved into pre-Adamites, death before the Fall, the history of disagreement among Church leaders on this issue, nor any number of controversies that one typically associates with the discussion of evolution and Latter-day Saint faith. My goal has been to try and give you one scientist's perspective on science and faith and why I personally find evolution to be faith-affirming. To be honest, I do not spend much time worrying about the mysteries.

I, of course, recognize that there are ideas in evolutionary theory that can be spun in such a way as to be in direct conflict with the doctrines of the Church, and unfortunately some prominent evolutionary biologists have gained great fame by doing so. Likewise, I recognize that there are interpretations of Latter-day Saint scripture that can be formulated in such a way as to contradict current ideas in evolutionary theory. What I would caution against is forcing a Joshua ultimatum here with "Choose you this day whom ye will serve" (Joshua 24:15), as if these are fundamentally and diametrically opposed views of creation with no degree of overlap and no possibility of reconciliation. In my experience, students who continue to think of this as a dichotomy will either have their faith so shaken when they learn the evidence for evolution that they drift away from the Church, or they will simply shut their eyes and their minds to what I consider to be a glorious way to view creation.

What we need to recognize is that we know very little about the Creation from either a religious or a scientific standpoint. Pitting these different perspectives against each other in a winner-takes-all cage fight seems perilous and something that I believe is not pleasing to the Lord. The Lord has not yet revealed the mechanics of creation: Doctrine and Covenants 101:32–34, quoted above, confirms this. And scientists are still probing around in the dark, the best we can, to try and understand even the basics of the creative process. In the meantime, I would suggest that it is best to be humble and grateful to live in a world that invokes such a feeling of awe and wonderment. I appreciate working at an institution that has been so supportive of my research in evolutionary biology. Much like Darwin, I believe there truly is grandeur in this view of life.

NOTES

1. Darwin, *On the Origin of Species by Means of Natural Selection, or the Preservation of Favoured Races in the Struggle For Life* (London: John Murray, 1860), 490.

2. See G. E. Hutchinson, "Homage to Santa Rosalia or Why Are There So Many Kinds of Animals," *American Naturalist* 93, no. 870 (May–June 1959), 146n.
3. The text of the packet is reprinted in William E. Evenson and Duane E. Jeffery, *Mormonism and Evolution: The Authoritative LDS Statements* (Salt Lake City: Greg Kofford Books, 2005). The packet's contents are also available online at http://whitinglab.byu.edu/PDF/Evolution%20 Packet.pdf.
4. Henry M. Morris, "The Testimony of Geologic History," http://www.the-highway.com/geologic-history_Morris.html.

INDEX

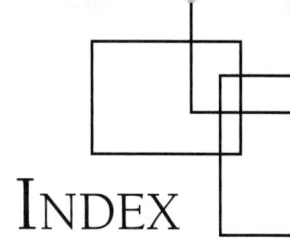

Abraham, 46–47, 137
Adam and Eve, 101–2, 114–15, 133. *See also* Fall of Adam
agency, 106
Alberty, Robert A., 6–7
alchemy, 27
Alma, 7, 8–9, 10, 32–33, 65–66
ambiguity, 82–84
American Psychological Association meeting, 86
animals, 134–35, 143–45
apostasy, 70–71
Arcturus, 44
Aristotle, 26–27, 63, 64, 155
astronomy: calendar keeping and, 47–55; scriptural references to, 37–47, 56–59; theories on, 26
Athanasian Creed, 69
Athanasius, 69
atmosphere, creation of, 139–41
atomic theory, 27
Augustine, St., 102–3, 116–17, 119
authority, appeal to, 63
Autrum, Hanjochem, 9
autumnal equinox, viii–ix

barley, 12–13
Barrow, Isaac, 102, 110
Bergin, Allen, 86
Bible: astronomical references in, 37–44, 46; calendar keeping in, 47–55; Newton on, 67
big bang theory, 115–18
birds, 143–44
block time, 106, 108
Book of Mormon, astronomical references in, 38–39, 43
Boötes, 44
Born, Max, 7
Brahe, Tycho, 63, 64
Brezhnev, Leonid, 4
Brigham Young University: balancing science and religion at, 2–3, 79–80, 82, 84–86; as best of all worlds, 90–91; future of, 89, 97–98; purpose of, 87
Brown, Rodney J., 80–81, 83–84
BYU. *See* Brigham Young University

calendar keeping, 47–55, 57–59
causality, 108
certainty, 5

Charles, King, 68
chittah, 12
choice, time as, 113–15
Christian colleges, 82–83. *See also* Brigham Young University
Church of Jesus Christ of Latter-day Saints, 19–22, 158–64
Clayton, William, 132
Conduitt, John, 61–62
continents, 141–42
Copernicus, 26, 64
Council in Heaven, 136
Cowdery, Oliver, 91
Creation: basic principles of, 123–27; conclusions on, 145; death before Fall and, 130–32; eternal nature of matter and, 135–36; fossils and, 132–34; introduction to, 123; LDS views on, 162–64; organic evolution and, 134–35; periods of, 128–29, 136–45, 146 (table); planning of, 136; studying, 164–66; timing of, 129–30
creationism, 162–64
creations of God: learning from, 19, 23–24; prove God's existence, 29
critical rationalism, 25
cumin, 11–12

Darwin, Charles, 151, 152, 156–57. *See also* evolution
data, spiritual, 8–9
David, 48
deadlines, 118
death, before Fall, 130–32
degrees of glory, 45
Democritus, 27
derivatives, 107
Derrick, David, 117–18
Descartes, René, 107
disease, miasma theory of, 28
disorder, law of increasing, 113–15
DNA, 165

Doctrine and Covenants: astronomical references in, 38, 42–43, 45; wheat and tares parable in, 70–71
Duchesne, Jules, 7

earth: age of, 129–30; creation of atmosphere, 139–41; organization of, 136–37; rotation of, 26, 38–39, 63; time and, 101–2. *See also* Creation; creations of God
eclipses, 40–41
Eddington, Arthur, 113–15
Einstein, Albert, vii, 25, 26, 104–5
empiricism, 25
Enos, 31–32
entomology, 151–52, 164
eternity, 116–18, 129, 135–36
Euler, Leonhard, 110
evidence, 95
evolution: conclusions on, 166–67; controversy over, 2, 79–80, 157–58; Creation and, 134–35; Darwin and, 156–57; introduction to, 151–53; Church and, 158–64; pattern and process in, 153–56; studying, 164–66. *See also* Darwin, Charles
ex nihilo creation, 163
experimentation, discovering truth through, 62–64
Eyring, Henry, 3, 7, 10
faith: Alma's experiment on, 65–66; defined, 7–8; learning by, 93–96; revelation through, 31–33; scientific method and, 3–13

Fall of Adam: death before, 130–32; law of increasing disorder and, 114–15; timing of, 129
farmer, parable of, 10–13
Farnsworth, Philo T., 3
First Presidency, 131, 133, 159–61
fitches, 11–12

INDEX

Fitzgerald, F. Scott, 22
Fletcher, Harvey, 3
fossils, 101–102, 131–33, 142
Friedrich, John, 5

Galileo, 64
Garden of Eden, 114. *See also* Adam and Eve; Fall of Adam
general apostasy, 70–71
Gjotterud, Ole, 6
glory of God, 81–82
God: belief in, 6–7; Creation and, 125–27; creations of, 19, 23–24; glory of, 81–82; Godhead and, 68–70; natural theology and, 155–56; Newton on, 64–66; omniscience of, 18–19; proving existence of, 29–30; time of, 111, 112–13, 115–17
Gödel, Kurt, 107
Godhead, 68–70
gold, 117–18
gospel, Restoration of, 72–74
Gregorian calendar, 59
Guth, Alan, 117

Haldane, J. B. S., 151–52
half-life, 130
Hawking, Stephen, 116–17
Hinckley, Gordon B., 125
Holmes, Arthur, 82–83
Holy Ghost: Godhead and, 68–70; learning through, viii; as witness, 8
Homo sapiens sapiens, 145
Hooke, Robert, 25
hope, faith and, 7–8
humility, 26, 33
Hunter, Howard W., 34
hydrogen, 138

increasing disorder, law of, 113–15
inflationary cosmology, 117
information: revealed, 31–33; spiritual, 8–9
insects, 151–52, 164
inspiration, 6. *See also* revelation
intelligence, 135–36. *See also* knowledge; learning
intelligent design, 163–64
intercalation, 52–53, 57–59
intuition, 6
ipse dixit, 63
Islamic calendar, 58–59
Israelites, calendar of, 47–55, 57–58

Jesus Christ: Godhead and, 68–70; tomb of, 95. *See also* Light of Christ
Jewish calendar, 47–55, 57–58

Kepler, Johannes, 63, 64
Kierkegaard, Søren, 81
Kimball, Spencer W., 89, 136
knowledge: gaining, 22–23; importance of, 21; missing, 82–84; partial, 22; search for, 80–81; through observation, 23–29; unity in, 87–89. *See also* learning
Kolob, 113

Laplace, Pierre Simon, 4
law(s): of increasing disorder, 113–15; of motion, 62, 113; spiritual and temporal, 90
learning: by faith and study, 93–96; importance of, 21; process for, 22–23; scientific and religious, 2–3; through Holy Ghost, viii; through observation, 23–29; through revelation, 31–33; unity in, 87–89. *See also* knowledge
Lee, Harold B., 94, 124
Leibniz, Gottfried, 110–11
Lewis, C. S., 111–12
life, definition, 134–35
light, creation of, 137–39

Light of Christ, 81–84
Lincoln, Abraham, 156
love, 88
lunar eclipses, 40–41
lunar months, 54, 57–59

Maeser, Karl G., viii
Malik, Charles H., 97–98
man, creation of, 145
manlike creatures, 133–34, 145
matter: eternal nature of, 135–36; theories on, 27
Maxwell, Neal A., 95
McConkie, Bruce R.: on Creation, 124, 126, 128; on revelation, 31
McConkie, Joseph, 91
McIntire, William, 132
Merrill, Joseph F., 2–3
Metonic cycle, 57–59
miasma theory of disease, 28
months, 51–53, 54, 57–59
Moody, J. Ward, vii
moon, 40–42, 142–43. *See also* lunar months; new moon
Morris, Henry, 163
Moses, 137
motion: laws of, 62, 113; time and, 109–11

natural theology, 155–156
Neanderthals, 133–34, 145
Nelson, Russell M., 3
Nephites, 38–39, 43
new moon, 47–55
Newton, Sir Isaac: on 1 John 5:7, 69–70; career of, vii, 67–68; conclusions on, 74; empiricism and, 25; on general apostasy, 70–71; on Godhead, 68–69; on God's existence, 64–66; in historical timeline, 64; introduction to, 61–62; on restoration, 72–74; on time, 110–11; on understanding scriptures, 66–67

Nibley, Hugh, 95–96, 133–34
Nieremberg, Juan Eusebio, 101
"now," 105–8
"now only," 108–9
nutmeg flower, 11–12

Oaks, Dallin H., 88, 90–91
observation: learning through, 23–29; of pattern and process, 154–56; predicting weather through, 39
Occam's razor, 110
oceans, 141–42
On the Origin of Species (Darwin), 156
organic evolution, 134–35
Orion, 44
oxygen, 140
ozone layer, 140

Packer, Boyd K., 22, 125
Palyi, Guyla, 17
Passover, 49
Pasteur, Louis, 28
pattern, process and, 154–56
Paul, 8, 9
Perelandra (Lewis), 111–12
personal revelation, 31–33
Phelps, William W., 129
plant life: creation of, 141–42; before Fall, 130–32; spiritual creation and, 134–35
Plato, 24–25, 64
Pleiades, 44
plowman, parable of, 10–13
Pointcaré, Henri, 110
Polkinghorne, John, 1
Popper, Karl, 25
premortal life, 136
Price, Huw, 103–4
process, pattern and, 154–56
Ptolemaic system, 26
Ptolemy, 26

radiometric dating, 129–30
rationalism, 24–25
Ray, John, 155–56
reality, 107, 109
reason versus revelation, 90–91
reconciliation, 92–93
relativity, 104–105
religion(s): education in, 84–86; focus of, 30–31; reconciliation among, 92–93; stability in, 56
respect for others' beliefs, 92–93
Restoration of gospel, 72–74
revelation: continuing, 82–83; Creation and, 126–27, 166; learning and, 23; versus reason, 90–91; as source of information, 31–33
Rhodes, Michael D., vii
rivers, 41
Roberts, Brigham H., 130–31
Romney, Marion G., 86, 94
Rydberg, Jan, 4, 5

Sabbath, 145
sacrifices, 50–51
St. Augustine, 102–3, 116–17, 119
science: education in, 79–80, 84–86; progress in, 24–28, 56
scientific atheism, 4–5
scientific method: discovering truth through, 25–28, 62–64; faith and, 3–13
scientific theism, 5–7
Scott, Richard G., 3
scriptures: astronomical references in, 37–47, 56–59; calendar-keeping references in, 47–55; Newton on, 66–67; proof for, 95; time in, 112–13
sea animals, 143–44
seasons, viii–ix, 143
Smith, George Albert, 2
Smith, Joseph: birth of, 156; on Creation, 132, 163; on eternal spirits and matter, 116; on God's creations, 18–19; on obtaining truth, 94; revelation given to, 91; on tolerance and love, 88
Smith, Joseph Fielding, 130–31
Smith, William, 129
Socrates, 24–25
solar eclipses, 40–41
solar system, creation of, 137–39
souls, 134–35
spiritual data, 8–9
spiritual laws, 90
spontaneous generation, 27–28
stars: counting, 46–47; creation of, 142–43
steady state theory, 115
stromatolites, 142
study, learning by, 93–94
Summerhays, Briant, vii
Summerhays, Hyrum Barrett, vii
sun, creation of, 142–143
sunrise, 40
"Systema Naturae," 155

Talmage, James E., 2, 124–25, 131
Taylor, John, 20, 88–89
technological advancements, 81–82
temple, Creation account in, 128
temporal laws, 90
theories: on beginning of time, 115–17, 118; of evolution, 153; evolution of scientific, 25–29
Thompson, J. J., 27
time: beginning of, 115–17, 118; as choice, 113–15; defined, 102–4; end of, 117–18; flow of, 111–13; heavenly bodies and, 143; introduction to, 101–2; as journey, 107–9; motion and, 109–11; as space, 104–6. *See also* calendar keeping
"today," 105–6, 108
tolerance, 88
total eclipses, 40–41
Trinity, 68–70

Triticum aestivum, 12
truth: eternal, 18–19; finding, 22–23, 25–29, 33–34, 80–81; John A. Widtsoe on, 93; Joseph Smith on obtaining, 94; Church and, 19–22; scientific and religious, viii, 123–24; through revelation, 31–33

"unfolding time," 108
unity, 87–89
universe, creation of, 136–37
University of Modena, 17–18
Ursa Major, 44
Ussher, James, 129

Van Fraassen, Bas C., 109
Venus, 142
vernal equinox, viii–ix

Waldman, Bernard, 5
water, 41, 138. *See also* oceans
weather, predicting, 39
Westphal, Wilhelm, 4–5
wheat, 12–13
wheat and tares, parable of, 70–71
Widtsoe, John A.: on Creation, 128; on God's creations, 24; on learning, 23; on science and religion, 3; on truth, 93
Worcester, Willis, 5–6

Young, Brigham: on science and religion, 19–20, 123–24; on teaching, viii; on truth, 18; on unity, 88